1996

Schooling, Welfare and Parental Responsibility

New Prospects Series

General Editors: Professor Ivor Goodson. Faculty of
                   Education. University of Western
                   Ontario. Canada and
                   Professor Andy Hargreaves. Ontario
                   Institute for Studies in Education.
                   Canada.

New Prospects Series 2

Schooling, Welfare and Parental Responsibility

Michael G. Wyness

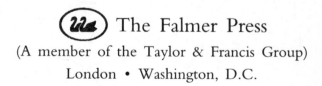 The Falmer Press

(A member of the Taylor & Francis Group)
London • Washington, D.C.

UK   The Falmer Press, 4 John Street, London WC1N 2ET
USA   The Falmer Press, Taylor & Francis Inc., 1990 Frost Road, Suite 101, Bristol, PA 19007

First published in 1996

A catalogue record for this book is available from the British Library

Library of Congress Cataloging-in-Publication Data are available on request

ISBN 0 7507 0437 3 cased
ISBN 0 7507 0438 1 paper

Jacket design by Caroline Archer

Typeset in 10/12 pt Bembo by
Graphicraft Typesetters Ltd., Hong Kong.

Printed in Great Britain by Burgess Science Press, Basingstoke on paper which has a specified pH value on final paper manufacture of not less than 7.5 and is therefore 'acid free'.

Contents

Acknowledgments

This book started life in the late 1980s as a doctoral thesis at the University of Edinburgh. I wish to thank a number of people for their intellectual, moral and financial support during this period: Sarah White, Graeme Morton, Suzanne Najam, Colin Bell, Charlie Rabb, Lynn Jamieson, Beverley Brown, Carl May, Tony Fallone and Keith Sharp. I must also mention here the parents, teachers and educationalists who took part in the study, and ESRC for funding the research.

More recent drafts have been read by colleagues at Nene under the usual academic pressures of heavy teaching and administrative work loads. I am eternally grateful to Jane Martin, Gordon Hughes, Wolgang Deike, Graham McBeath, Andy Pilkington and Chris Winch. Finally, I would like to thank Andy Hargreaves for his support.

This book is dedicated to my parents, George and Kathleen, and to Flaming Kate.

Introduction

The convergence of public order policy and educational reform in Britain has generated compelling, if inconsistent, images of the 'responsible parent'. On the one hand, parental responsibilities are invoked as legitimate socializing powers set against the 'collectivist' influence of the educational establishment. On the other hand, these same responsibilities are implicated as part of an ever-tightening alleged causal chain which links delinquency and child abuse to inadequate parenting. What we are not offered are realistic images of how the parents themselves routinely negotiate what Bronfenbrenner (quoted in Popenoe 1988, p. 330) calls the 'enduring irrational emotional involvement' with children.

Current public anxieties over family life reflect the way that social commentators and politicians trade on common sense in identifying these conflicting impressions of parental responsibilities. Many of these anxieties can also be detected in the more academic literature on parental decline. This book assesses these common-sense and academic assumptions which collectively constitute the 'idea' of a parent's responsibilities from the point of view of parents themselves.

The idea of the parent as both victim of state intervention and perpetrator of moral neglect has its origins in the wider political and social structures. It also originates at the agency level from those with a professional interest in the welfare of both parents and children. Welfare agencies find themselves in a similar double bind situation. Social workers and teachers are both charged with interfering in family affairs and called to account in the assessments of parental culpability.[1] A second aim of the book, then, is to assess the role that these 'welfare' agencies play in the constitution of parental responsibilities. In particular, I adopt a case-study approach in identifying the welfare responsibilities of the teaching profession. In the process, I examine the grounded assumptions that teachers make about parents and assess the quality of relations between the home and the school.

In this brief introduction I set out the arguments addressed in the book. But first I must address the relevance of teaching as a welfare profession: for the boundary between the home and 'welfare' has been sharpened recently by concern expressed about the 'interventionist' role of the social services. Dingwall *et al.* (1983) point to a dilemma in social work by suggesting an inverse relationship between the success of the state in underwriting the welfare of the child and the well-being of the family.

> They [the social services] cannot be given the legal power to underwrite
> an investigative form of surveillance without destroying the liberal family.

1

At the same time, the state cannot opt out. There is a collective interest in the moral and physical wellbeing of future citizens, in the quality of social reproduction, as a necessary condition for the survival of this particular type of society. (p. 220)

Social workers have inevitably become the target of critics of the welfare state; perhaps because of the highly visible nature of the intrusion into the family in the interests of the child's welfare; perhaps because the social services are depicted as playing a surrogate parental role in child rearing when family breakdown occurs. What is significant here is the idea that the state makes collective claims on the child's well-being. Whether these claims supersede the individualistic 'rights' of parents is a question which informs the discussions with the parents and teachers.[2]

The apparently intractable relationship between parents and 'welfare' agencies cannot be so easily applied to relations between the home and the school. The intemperate tone of the polemic against social work, sometimes suggests that the very existence of social work as a profession is at stake. State provision of schooling, on the other hand, does not produce the same degree of apoplexy among the state's detractors; possibly because it is commonly accepted that the school has a legitimate pedagogic role to play in child development.[3] Critics of the state education system have focused on the welfarist ethos which allegedly pervades schooling. The *Black Papers* (Cox and Dyson, 1971), an early influential critique, offers a sustained attack on the state and education. Educationalists on the political right argue that there is a need to restructure parent–teacher relations according to free market principles because of the perception that the school does not act in the best interests of the parent as consumer. The teaching profession, according to its critics, is imbued by collectivist, 'permissive' principles which undermine the responsibility and authority of the individual parent (Cox and Dyson, 1971).

Two points flow from this critique. First, the development of a welfare network in school is often taken as evidence of the 'abusive' powers of local education authorities and the teaching profession because it draws parents into a more dependent relationship with the teaching staff and underpins the dominant teaching assumption that parents, particularly of the working-class variety, are an obstacle in the teaching process. In Chapter 3 I assess the kinds of assumptions that parents and teachers make about their respective 'spheres of influence'. More specifically, I draw on the accounts of a sample of teachers with pastoral responsibilities in illustrating the mental maps that teachers have of the relationship between the home and the school. I then go on to assess the ways that these ideas underpin their encounters with parents.

A second point relates to teaching practice. Teachers who linked problems that children had in school primarily to factors located outside of the teaching context would presumably tend to overcompensate for children from 'problem' backgrounds when fulfilling their teaching responsibilities in class (Sharp and Green, 1975). Notions of 'standards' which are continually invoked by critics of the education system do not simply refer to the content of education. They refer also to the way teachers deliver the curriculum in terms of classroom discipline.

The teachers in this study, as well as mediating between the home and the school, have more conventional classroom teaching responsibilities. They are thus well placed to comment on both the influence the school has on the home and any impact that home–school relations might have on teaching practice. Chapter 2, then, deals with the extent to which the managerial skills of the teacher in class are necessarily diluted by a teaching approach that emphasizes the emotional and social as well as the intellectual welfare of the child.

Chapters 4 and 5 shift from the 'educational' to a parental frame of reference by drawing on the accounts offered by a sample of working-class and middle-class parents. This is not simply a shift from the professional to the personal. For notions of 'education' and 'welfare' structure the understandings that parents have of their own responsibilities towards their children. I originally started from the premise that what parents and teachers do are fundamentally different. In Chapters 4 and 5 I document the ways in which parents assert their moral and social responsibilities in and against what is perceived to be an increasingly morally and socially fragmented outside world. In the process parents often invoke the influence, the skills and the superior knowledge of the school in constructing for themselves a sphere of responsibility. The relationship between the home and the school, then, does not neatly dovetail with an implicit division of responsibility between the home and the school.

In Chapter 4, I concentrate on the routine business of setting up boundaries within the home that often necessitate setting up boundaries between the home and the outside world. Discipline and control are concepts that structure the daily business of classroom teaching. These concepts also routinely structure the responsibilities that parents have for their children's welfare. They are delineated in Chapter 4.

In Chapter 5, the debate around the interventionist powers of the school as a moral agency are more explicitly addressed in referring to responsibilities for sex education. Questions of imputed parental responsibility can be tested empirically through the accounts that parents and teachers give of their experiences in educating children and pupils in sexual matters. More fundamentally, sex education can be used to illustrate the possibilities open to schools for underwriting the welfare of children which do not necessarily undermine the sense that parents have of their own skills in supervising their children's moral welfare.

The concluding chapter locates the major findings of the book within the conflicting images of parenthood offered at the beginning of this introduction. Parental responsibilities here are constructed out of two competing conceptions of parenthood which reflect quite different ideological emphases in public policy.

In this book, then, I locate assumptions and explanations held about child rearing and child support at a level which is meaningful to parents and teachers. For what parents and teachers say matters. Yet, the academic and political agenda is set by a general state of affairs that makes assumptions about the average parent and the average teacher. In the following chapter, I outline an ongoing debate within academia that converges on the theme of family decline. In one sense this notion of decline is being tested through the accounts that both parent and teachers give of their respective social worlds. In another sense, the micro level of analysis allows for

the terms of the debate, terms that reflect to some extent public policy pronouncements, to be translated by those interviewed into their own working vocabulary of
practices.

Notes

1   A recent headline in the *London Evening Standard* ran 'How the state stole our sons', 7th
    January, 1993.
2   An implicit individualism runs through this model of home–school relations, what Morgan
    (1985) terms 'methodological familism'. The family is articulated as a single unit in rela-
    tion to the outside world. The family in a rhetorical and political sense takes on the same
    characteristics as the 'individual' where arguments are put forward for the restriction of
    'collectivist' trends in society (Mount, 1982).
3   This is not to say that there has always been a consensus over the necessity for compulsory
    education. In the late nineteenth century, conflict was rife between parents and the state
    over the introduction of compulsory education, See Donzelot, 1979; David, 1980; Jamieson,
    1987. More recently, the alleged increase in school absence has suggested that the taken-
    for-granted compulsory nature of schooling is now being questioned (Carlen, Gleeson
    and Wardhaugh, 1992).

Chapter 1

The Home, the School and State Intervention

Introduction

In the first part of this chapter I draw on an ideologically and politically disparate group of scholarly work which converges around the theme of 'decline'. In more general terms this decline refers to the Weberian notion of disenchantment, with family disorganization taken as the primary indicator of moral decline. Decline here refers to social changes which undermine the importance and the resilience of parents.

What I take to be the 'decline thesis' in this chapter is composed of three frameworks of intervention. Although they can be viewed as quite different, possibly even incompatible models of 'social control', I go on to argue in the second part of the chapter that they suffer from similar empirical and theoretical shortcomings. The first model defines loss of parental authority as a consequence of more powerful external influences replacing the social and moral roles of parents. In another sense, decline refers to the gradual replacement of 'natural', 'traditional' powers with more externally defined responsibilities which at best keep parents permanently on the defensive, at worst disorient and alienate parents. A final way of understanding 'decline' is to question the common basis upon which a theory of family life is erected. In most instances the modern family presupposes a public–private dichotomy that counterpoises the 'natural' personal skills and rights that parents have with the powers of various child support agencies. Rather than being seen as a timeless, natural state of being, parenthood and by implication 'the family' is a product of relatively recent social and political change. Within this context, the education system arguably plays a formative rather than destructive role in the process of maintaining strategic control over at the very least, working-class life.

The second part of this chapter also offers an assessment by focusing on the methodological as well as theoretical shortcomings. This is then used as the basis for outlining my own empirical approach to the problem as well as offering a rationale for the sampling frame.

Welfare and Family Life: Supplanting the Parent

Intervention can be read as a simple historical transfer of socializing powers from parents to outside sources. The resurrection of the family by modernists such as

Parsons and Bales (1956) and Fletcher (1966) was countered by conservatives such as Riesman (1950), Bronfenbrenner (1970) and the Bergers (1983) in the United States, Popenoe (1988) in Sweden, Meyer (1977) in France, and Mount (1982) in Britain, who argue that parental authority is under threat from a variety of external sources ranging from the state to the peer group. Parental authority in these terms is seen as a necessarily private locus of social and psychological resources, which parents draw on ensuring that their children develop moral characters. Any movement from the outside into this private realm is argued to have a deleterious effect on relations between parents and children.

Within this locus of external intervention, the school is argued to play a prominent part. The Bergers, in characteristically polemical style, argue that the family has now lost its primary moral functions to the education system (1983, p. 191). Whereas sometime in the late nineteenth century the school only reaffirmed the values that were transmitted within the family unit, it is now attempting to set itself up as the only moral frame of reference which would render the authority that parents have less effective.

Christopher Lasch takes up this theme by arguing that the school is now imbued with anti-intellectual ideas that undermine the division between 'education' and 'socialisation' (1979, p. 239). The intellectual content of the curriculum has been diluted by the demands of what Lasch calls 'life adjustments'. Pupils learn about practical experiential things that Lasch argues are normally passed on by parents. Lasch quotes statements made by 'leading educationalists' from the early part of the century:

> Social political and industrial changes have forced upon the school responsibilities formerly laid upon the home. Once the school had mainly to teach the elements of knowledge, now it is charged with the physical, mental and social training of the child as well. (1979, p. 268)

A key parental responsibility that incorporates 'physical, mental and social training' is sex education. I discuss this in more detail in Chapter 5. But it is worth mentioning at this stage that the recent debate over sex education is framed along the same lines as the decline thesis.[1] Critics like Thomas Szasz, set up an antagonistic relationship between the school's moral functions and the idea that sex education is a parental responsibility because parents are best suited to take 'care and control of the sexual life of (their) children' (1980, p. 153). He argues that the systematic introduction of a sex education curriculum in schools has taken away a parental right to introduce moral and sexual matters to their children.

Riesman (1950) more systematically focuses on the ways that schooling undermines parental authority through what we might consider the legitimate practice of classroom teaching. According to Riesman, in the earlier historical period of 'inner-direction' the teacher had a formal pedagogic relationship with the pupil that was scrupulously separate from the more affective ties the children had with their parents.

> Seating . . . is arranged formally . . . The walls are decorated with the ruins of Pompeii and the bust of Caesar. For all but the few exceptional children

who can transcend the dead forms of their classical education and make the dead forms come alive, these etchings and statues signify the irrelevance of the school to the emotional problems of the child. The teacher herself has neither the understanding of nor the time for these emotional problems, and the child's relation to other children enters her purview only in disciplinary cases. (1950, p. 58)

The implication here is that the emotional needs of the child can more appropriately be dealt with within the home. This division of labour between the school and the home separates out the affective from the instrumental, the moral from the intellectual. It thus reduces any confusion that might result in the mind of the child from the potentially competitive nature of the relationship between the school and the home, if the former attempts to provide a more socio-moral frame of reference.

Riesman argues that the division of labour broke down in the modern period of 'other-direction'. He cites the changing physical environment of the classroom which now engenders greater informality in pupil–pupil and pupil–teacher relations. He goes on to argue that the spatial organization of the classroom changes as pupils no longer sit in individualized spaces. They are more likely to be placed with other groups of children who, rather than displaying similar intellectual capacities, are grouped together according to how well they get on with each other; 'human relations' enters the classroom. As Riesman states, 'where to sit becomes problematical – a clue to one's location on the friendship chart' (1950, p. 61).

The human relations analogy is further extended as the teacher is more concerned with the 'management' of the classroom than any unilateral exercise of penal disciplinary forms. Lines of communication cross through the teacher as attempts are made to engender cooperative, rather than competitive, relations between pupils. Teachers in these terms become focal points for expression of 'public opinion' (Riesman, 1950, p. 62). Ultimately, the intellectual skills which were previously installed in individual pupils are argued to have been displaced through this managerial approach.

This model of intervention, then, suggests that progressive teaching practices need to be seen within the context of an education system which is now imbued with liberal ideas about 'socializing' the child. The new teaching ethic extends the teacher's pedagogic responsibilities into the realms of psychology and social work. Teachers are more concerned with associating educational failure with inadequate parenting. Teachers no longer play the role of pedagogue because their responsibilities extend into the home in the search for solutions to educational failure as a social rather than educational problem.

The Structuring of Parental Responsibilities

Rather than the school eclipsing the home as a primary social and moral reference for children, a second interpretation of intervention emphasizes the responsibilities that replace parents' traditional powers. Lasch (1979) and Harris (1983) argue that external agencies are influential in the way that they actively encourage parents to take responsibility for their children's well-being. Not only is the state involved in the assertion of parental responsibilities, it is actively supervising them. There is, here, an element of both giving and taking away. The state through the school and the social services is constantly supervising the child-rearing capacities of the parent. This means intervening by taking away 'natural' parental skills whilst at the same time encouraging parents to take more responsibility for their children's well-being. According to Harris and Lasch, this leads not only to powerlessness, but a more generalized anxiety.

Both authors link this anxiety to changes in the social structure which has led to intrusions into the home. Lasch refers to the 'proletarianization of parenthood': the same changes which have deprived the work force of their 'craft' skills, are having a similar impact within the home. This is echoed by Harris.

> Childraising becomes a technical task judged by the effects it achieves. Parents, like other producers, are judged by the quality of their products. (1983, p. 241)

Harris outlines the way teachers, among others, put pressures on parents to 'turn out' their children. Parents particularly mothers, are seen by teachers to be responsible for their children in an unconditional sense. Independently of any notion that misbehaviour in school might be a consequence of inadequate teaching, parents are encouraged to believe they are responsible for the misbehaviour. The child's behaviour in public becomes an indicator of the parent's technical performance. Apart from the pressure this puts parents under to get things right, parents are deprived of the means needed to achieve success in child rearing.

Lasch makes the same point with reference to the influence of Dr Spock. Lasch applauds Spock's reversal of his earlier advocacy of 'permissiveness' to encouraging parents to be 'authoritarian' and to take responsibility (1979, pp. 280–4). Yet, this position is also criticized. Lasch argues that Dr Spock now tells parents that their authority is sacrosanct whilst simultaneously undermining their capacity to exercise this authority by 'reminding them of the incalculable consequences of their actions' (1977, p. 172).

Lasch expands on this point in *The Culture of Narcissism*. Implicit in the demands on parents to recapture their authority is the model of the 'perfect parent' (1979, pp. 291–2). The latter is the a-social anthropological 'mother of more patterned societies', whose consummate relationship with nature is one which modern parents can never hope to emulate. The irony for Lasch is that any biologically based or naturally given notion of authority cannot by definition be culturally prescribed.[2]

For Lasch, then, the central problem for parents is that they are deprived of their 'natural' powers by professionals and then encouraged by the same people to take responsibility for their children's present and future well-being. This is not simply the replacement of the maternal instinct with 'therapeutic' solutions. Where parents are deprived of their responsibilities, Lasch identifies two scenarios: at best, parents act directly on behalf of state-sponsored agencies of control where they have little decision-making powers; at worst, parents are totally deprived of any role in the rearing of their children. The problem for Lasch is more complex in that the therapeutic solution incorporates the notion that parents are central actors in the process of socialization.

> Having first declared parents incompetent to raise their offspring without professional help, social pathologists 'gave back' the knowledge they had appropriated – gave it back in a mystifying fashion that rendered parents more helpless than ever, more abject in their dependence on expert opin-ion. (Lasch, 1977, p. 18)

Harris (1983) identifies more immediate problems for parents which reflect the ways in which the school is able to exercise control over their own lives as well as their children's. Parental control, according to Harris, becomes increasingly more difficult where children spend proportionately less time within the domestic pur-view. It becomes impossible to restrict children's movements because they are expected to spend proportionately more time away from their parents at school and with friends. Parents' problems are further compounded by the kinds of messages they pick up about how their children relate to their teachers. Harris argues that teachers encourage children to break down the traditional generational differences in status by acting as confidantes rather than authority figures (1983, p. 239). The concept of control assumes that parents are forced to adopt a more hierarchical role in keeping their children within their purview. This goes against what he terms 'the dominant child-rearing ideology' where authority is downplayed in favour of close-ness and equality. Within this context, parents appear to have all the responsibil-ity without any of the concomitant power. Whereas the school, because it reflects the dominant child-rearing ideology and because of its legitimate role in providing knowledge and skills, appears to have all the power and is able to attribute problems in the classroom to inadequate parenting.

Social Constructionism and Maternal Responsibility

The previous models of intervention focus on the way that external agencies, such as the school, have an impact on family life. There is an implicit essentialism here in the way that 'natural', 'traditional' skills have been refashioned as 'responsibilities' by external sources. Furthermore, this essentialism is reinforced in the way that these influences are seen as alien and mystifying – having a negative effect both on par-ents' sense of self and their ability to take care of their children.

Adopting a more 'social constructionist' approach would require moving away from identifying the essential nature of the 'socializing' role of parents and the 'educational' role of teachers. If we refer to the work of the French school of social constructionism, namely Ariés (1960), Donzelot (1979) and Badinter (1980), the conceptual framework which posits an oppositional relationship between the private and the public is abandoned in favour of what Deleuze, in the preface to *Policing of Families*, calls a 'hybrid domain – the social' (Donzelot, 1979, p. x).

Lasch and Harris have both identified the way the school and other 'caring professions' inadequately attempt to shore up the boundary between the school and the outside world. But the lack of success here is due, quite simply, to the impossibility of agencies being able to replace or reconstruct the private space upon which family life is built. Donzelot, on the other hand, has a quite different view of the relationship between the family and the outside world. His thesis is not simply a story of the rescue of the family by the welfare state. Rather, Donzelot was

> positing the family, not as a point of departure, as a manifest reality, but as a moving resultant, an uncertain form whose intelligibility can only come from studying the system of relations it maintains with the sociopolitical level. (1977, p. xxv)

The modern family here is not some essentially private locus of values and morality which had been intruded upon by alien external forces. The French school documented the development of a discourse which focused on the responsibilities that mothers ought to have for the protection and nurturing of children. For Donzelot, the idea of the modern family grew out of this discourse.

Early twentieth-century versions of this discourse focused on relations between the family and the school. There were several prominent elements. Debates took place over universal education. On the one side there were the elitists who saw this in terms of the collapsing of distinctions between 'good' and 'bad' schools (Donzelot, 1979, p. 203). On the other side there were those who saw the school as a means by which delinquency might be regulated.[3] Donzelot also documented the introduction of educational psychology, parent associations and parent schools as the state moved towards strengthening links between the family and the school.

The key to the synthesizing of what Donzelot termed familial and educational norms was the introduction of the confessional technique in school (1979, p. 209). Problems that children had in school were to be thoroughly dissected in discussions between mothers and teachers. Mothers were to be encouraged to divulge all their family secrets about their relations with their children. Mothers were also encouraged to supervise their children's time at home in an effort to detect any signs that might indicate the source of the problem (*ibid.*, p. 206). Ultimately, the teacher/councillor was to encourage mothers to take responsibility for these problems through improving the communication that they have with their children; by ceding to their children's demands and by uncovering their children's true desires. The school thus became an important means through which mothers were able to understand, moralize and socialize their children.

The more traditional models of intervention and the French school of social constructionism are by no means mutually exclusive. The replacement of parental authority with an allegedly weaker set of responsibilities can be read as the replacement of a patriarchal authority with a maternal responsibility. Harris' corollary of the 'anxious mother' converges on the way that the 'public gaze' for Donzelot falls particularly on the mother. Yet there is one crucial difference here. Lasch discusses variations of the mother-centred family in pathological terms. 'Momism' and the matrifocal black family are linked to the rise in youthful disaffection and delinquency. Donzelot, on the other hand, delineates the way that the mother-centred family was constructed through the convergence of social, economic and intellectual forces as a means of regulating working-class children and solving the recurrent problem of delinquency. Donzelot argues that the French education system in the early twentieth century was instrumental in the development of a maternal responsibility.

Walkerdine (1990), from a British perspective, adopts a similar approach in identifying this process as a form of 'covert regulation'. Focusing on mothers of young children, Walkerdine argues that the idea of a maternal responsibility suggests that mothers are held accountable for their children because of a middle-class model of 'normal' child development that filters through the schools. A pathology of inadequate socialization is constructed through this covert regulation in class that implicated working-class mothers by encouraging them to believe that they are responsible for their children's educational failings. Walkerdine's analysis is interesting because it turns the traditional conception of decline on its head. Following Sharp and Green (1975) the liberationist (in traditional terms 'permissive') potential of child-centredness obscures the subtle ways through which children are controlled. The monitoring of the 'whole child' at 'the child's own pace' is taken as part of an ever tightening system of checks and controls within which the child is placed.

In Chapter 2 I take up Walkerdine's position in more detail when delineating the role of the school and the individual teacher within a welfare network. In the following passages I want to assess the common themes that run through these models of intervention in more critical terms. These arguments focus on the conjunction of social and political change and the development of the caring professions. Notions of 'welfare' and the 'tutelary complex' converge on the family by redefining and restructuring domestic relations according to external and culturally alien norms. Family relations are opened up for public scrutiny, generating dependency relations that conflict with the way parents internalize their roles as responsibilities. The decline thesis presents us with a range of sophisticated and provocative readings of the condition of modern family life. But there is little empirical evidence to substantiate the negative effects these external sources have on parents. Furthermore, there is little to suggest that the 'average' parent is wholly reliant on the state for bringing up their children in terms of how the daily routine business of bringing up children has been dramatically affected. From the point of view of those involved in the 'intrusions', there is also little empirical detail on how teachers, social workers and educational welfare officers undermine the authority that parents have.

These critiques of the state also suggest that the modern family has been increasingly subjected to a series of 'social controls'. Whether this is conceptualized in terms of the 'de-skilling' of parenthood or a discourse on parenthood, parents are argued to have a much weaker sense of their own authority and have fewer spaces within which to make meaningful decisions on their children's future. Despite Lasch's desire 'to convince the reader that the contemporary family is the product of human agency, not of abstract social "forces"', what we have here is the essential nature of family life determined, more or less, by professional and institutional agencies of 'social control' (Lasch, 1977, p. xx).

The structural notion of determinacy, in one sense, is much weaker in Donzelot's work. For he suggests a more contingent relationship between the various social forces that converged on the family. Nevertheless, there is little sense in which 'human action' in the form of resistance, rejection or strategy were prominent features of family life. With the exception of Harris' work on the emotional consequences of 'intervention' for the family, there is little analysis of the ways in which parents responded to the overtures of the various agents of the state (Giddens, 1991, p. 177). Given the complex and sometimes contradictory nature of these agencies' actions, we cannot simply infer a blanket interventionist or policing role from some all-encompassing notion of welfarism (Dingwall, Eekelaar and Murray, 1983). Apart from tendencies towards 'professionalization' and 'bureaucratization', there is little sense of commitment or conviction from those agents of the state who are argued to determine the nature of family life. As Dingwall *et al.* argue, presenting the social worker, the teacher or the local doctor as 'agents of social control presents a one-dimensional picture of a subtle reality' (*ibid.*, p. 210).

Lay Social Theories

What is missing from these accounts, then, is rigorous empirical analysis that not only addresses the mechanisms for defining a parent's responsibility and the consequences this has for the parent, but attends to the perceptions of other key actors most closely involved in this process. In this book, I address the different ways in which both parents and teachers make sense of their respective roles and responsibilities. I also outline the understandings that both parents and teachers have of the intersection of their respective social worlds. Parent and teacher talk comes in the form of accounts generated from interview data.[4]

The analytical focus for these accounts is a body of grounded knowledge, a set of common-sense ideas that parents and teachers hold about their present circumstances and future orientations. From the interviews with parents and teachers I elicit what Dingwall *et al.* (*ibid.*, p. 56) call lay social theories. These are defined as:

> commonsense, practical guide(s) which we can consult to make sense of everyday occurrences and to formulate appropriate responses.

The lay social theory comes close to Berger and Luckmans' (1968) 'recipe knowledge' and Gubrium and Holsteins' (1990, p. 143) 'native theorizing' in that the framework of ideas and meanings that people draw on is a 'working' knowledge immediately applicable to everyday situations. Although there is a temptation to counterpoise this kind of knowledge with the more sophisticated knowledge generated by social scientists, more recent work has suggested that the lay person relies more and more on the conceptual frameworks provided by social scientists as a way of coping with the uncertainties associated with 'post-modern' routines (Giddens, 1991). Nevertheless, the lay social theory can be clearly delineated according to three distinct characteristics. First of all, this knowledge is rooted in immediate and practical experience – what Giddens calls 'practical consciousness' (1984, p. xxii). This knowledge is in turn framed within more generalizable understandings of the way in which the social world is organized. A third feature is the normative and prescriptive tone of these statements which gives them an immediate but general understanding of the way the world is. Lay social theories, then, in this book, are both moral statements and explanations of the professional and social worlds expressed by teachers and parents which reflect the practical understandings they have of social problems that are routinely confronted.

It follows from this theoretical emphasis that the research techniques were largely 'qualitative' with an emphasis on indepth interviewing. Enough has been said about the methodological implications of interviewing,[5] but I will briefly make two points here. First, the interview, if approached carefully and sensitively, is an effective technique in constructing theories about practices not normally amenable to more traditional research approaches. Parents and teachers were, accordingly, allowed a degree of latitude in accounting for their own social worlds. Second, to some extent I tried to naturalize the interview as an 'encounter' (Goffman, 1972). The interviews allowed me to corroborate what the teachers and parents were saying as their accounts unfolded much in the same way as in any conversation where both parties periodically check the internal consistency of the accounts that they hear. But I was also able to counter the dangers of over empathizing with respondents by establishing at the outset that I was interested in documenting and analyzing the respondents' social worlds. The researcher has a quite specific role to play in documenting and analyzing social life.[6]

The interviews with the teachers are contextualized in the following chapter and also discussed in Appendix 2. In interviewing the parents I might have chosen to interview the mothers and fathers together. However, I decided to interview them separately for two reasons. Firstly, I take Laing and Estersons' (1970) methodological injunction seriously – they believe that treating interviews with family members together as if they counted as observational data does not really bring us any closer to understanding the family routine.[7] Any attempt at presenting the family, in the words of Burgess (1926), as a 'unity of interacting personalities' is restricted where the interaction being observed takes place as part of a dialogue with an 'outsider', the researcher. Secondly, any attempts at contextualizing interviews with family members as if they counted as observation data, need to be offset by the advantages of 'privacy' in characterizing the interview between researcher and respondent (Allan, 1980). Interviewing mothers and fathers together, then, would have inhibited either parent from answering questions fully and freely, especially where the questions concerned the topics of power, authority and sexuality within the home. On this basis, I interviewed parents separately in their homes.

Targeting the Parental Sample

In this final part, I provide a rationale for the parental sample on the basis of three key variables: social class, age of the children, and the gender of the parents targeted. (The specific details of the parents interviewed can be found in Appendix 2.)

Class

Debates around the decline of the family tend to presuppose a particular family form.[8] Riesman, Lasch, and the Bergers, in reasserting parental authority over other external sources of support, eulogise the middle-class form in that parents are no longer able to produce the bourgeois individual. Donzelot's analysis of nineteenth-century French society compares the middle-class and working-class family forms. But his argument falls back on the 'trickle down' theory where social change is reduced to the embourgeoisement of family life; the twentieth century being presented as the dominance of a bourgeois-privatized family form.[9]

Harris' work is more promising in that, by looking at the emotional interior of the family, he argues that we cannot deduce the precise form that family relations take from the mode of production (1983, p. 244). Yet, there is little to suggest that any family members are able to escape the proletarianizing effects of late capitalism.[10] The work of Zaretsky (1982) and Holman (1988), on the other hand, is instructive in identifying the class-based nature of welfare consumption and state activity. Zaretsky criticizes the proletarianization thesis by arguing that any marxist theory of the family needs to distinguish the character of family life along social class lines (1982, p. 190). Holman, following Walkerdine, focuses on the way in which the state targets the poorest families for intervention.

Research that focuses more specifically on the links between parents and teachers tends to suggest that middle-class parents have a structural affinity with the schooling system (Bernstein, 1975; Newsons, 1976). Unencumbered by the community and the subculture, middle-class parents are able to direct their children into middle-class and professional positions by taking advantage of the post-war expansion in education. Little is said about how these structural affinities were played out in the form of contacts and networks with teachers. Little is said about the quality of relations between parents and teachers.

Sharp and Greens' (1975) analysis of child-centred teaching practices draws on accounts from both parents and teachers. Yet, the focus is on relations between parents and teachers in a 'deprived' working-class area. This work still begs two questions: is the adoption of a child-centred approach as much a product of the social geography of the community as any deep seated commitment to a particular teaching philosophy? If not, how might a child-centred approach in a middle-class school influence the quality of relations between the teachers and parents? Lareau (1989), writing within a North American context, does not directly address these questions. But in her ethnographic analysis of parents and teachers in a middle-class and working-class area she does provide more qualitative evidence to back up the general trend in the sociology of education, mentioned earlier, by suggesting that access to cultural capital determines the quality of relations between parents and teachers. Ownership for middle-class parents strengthens their affinities with teachers. As in Connell *et al.*'s (1982) notion of 'mutual mistrust' between the working-class home and the school, Lareau argues that the absence of cultural capital produces 'separateness' – parent–teacher relations here characterized by anxiety, mistrust and miscommunication.

I have argued that we need to go beyond the macro level in uncovering both the quality of relations between parents and teachers and the 'mental maps' that they both draw on in making sense of their responsibilities. Apart from the size of the parental sample, the exploratory nature of this approach limits the generation of statistical correlations. Nevertheless, the inclusion of a stratified sample according to social class is a useful starting point in identifying the parents to be interviewed. From time to time the data is used to highlight possible differences between working-class and middle-class parents.

Age

The parental sample was also defined in terms of the stage the parents had reached in the family lifecycle. First, I take up the point made by Graham Allan (1985, p. 42) that very little work has been done on the parenting of adolescent children. It may be that child rearing is seen to be a more complete and unconditional responsibility in early childhood for parents (Ribbens, 1993, p. 82). It may be that parent-hood or motherhood at this stage of the family lifecycle conforms more precisely to the dominant concept of 'socialization' which suggests a linear and deterministic relationship between the parent and child. I also suggested in my review of the decline thesis, that research and analysis on child rearing tends to focus on parenting in the early years because this period is taken to be the most formative in the life of the parent and the child.

This book addresses these issues empirically by drawing on data from parents of adolescent children. In Chapter 4 I first assess the ways in which parents attempt to balance the demands made on themselves as carers and the need to allow their children a degree of adolescent autonomy. There is here the suggestion of a more dynamic relationship between parent and child. At the same time, I argue that parents still have a significant 'formative' influence during this period. Secondly, early indications from the teaching sample suggested that 14- and 15-year-old children were the most difficult to manage in the classroom. Given that the book is concerned with the ways that teachers 'explain' problem children with reference to the roles parents play, it made sense to focus on this age range in the interviews with teachers. Given also that there is an implicit comparative frame of reference between parenting and teaching it was important to interview parents with children at this 'difficult' age. Thirdly, the 14 to 15 age bracket was important because it was the point where parents took a formal 'educational' responsibility for their children's future school career.

Chapter 3 assesses the quality of parent–teacher relations by focusing on the subject choice process which gave parents and teachers the opportunity to discuss the future academic careers of the children.

Gender

I mentioned earlier that the paucity of sociological research on parents and adolescents reflects an over-emphasis on the early formative period of child rearing. This may also account for the neglect of the fathering role with researchers tending to assume that it is mothers who play the formative role in the early years. I return to this theme in Chapters 4 and 5. A brief comment is necessary here in establishing the possibility of the father playing a more formative role.

From the earlier discussion on the rise of the concept of parental responsibility, the decline thesis identifies the loss of paternal power and authority as a major source of moral decline and confusion. There is no need to rehearse the well-worn theme of the 'absence' of the father figure. What is being argued by Lasch, Donzelot and, more recently, Dennis and Erdos (1993) is that problems parents have with their children are a direct consequence of the gradual replacement of paternal authority with an allegedly weaker form of maternal responsibility. In Chapter 5 I question the assumptions made about the marginal role that fathers play in child rearing. Furthermore, the marginal role of the father is argued to be a consequence of parents becoming more open to external sources of influence and support with mothers being specifically targeted by welfare agencies and the 'therapeutic' community.[11] I assess this in Chapters 3 and 5 by drawing on the lay social theories and general perceptions that teachers have of the respective roles of mothers and fathers.

Notes

1   Although sex education would appear to be a fundamental aspect of socialization in most societies, it is less of a public issue in some countries. According to Goldman and Goldman (1982, p. 70), Sweden has a more open approach to 'discussions on sex' and a public consensus over sex education in schools.
2   This point is discussed in more detail in my review of Anderson, D. (1988) *Full Circle? Bringing Up People in the Post-Permissive Society* (Wyness, 1990).
3   David (1980) has produced a useful text on these developments in Britain.
4   The methodological problem of separating 'teaching' and 'parenting' from teachers with children who were interviewed is discussed in Appendix 1.
5   See Wyness, 1994b, for a review of these implications.
6   In Bott's (1964, pp. 19–20) case her research was hampered by being perceived by some of her respondents as both confidante and therapist.
7   There are, of course, serious cultural limitations on doing a full ethnography of family life. See Wyness (1996, forthcoming).
8   See Bernardes (1985) and Gittins (1985) for a critique of the 'universal' nuclear family.
9   See Lynn Jamieson, 1987, for an extended critique of this.
10 This is evident from an earlier paper where Harris distinguished between two family types, the 'disintegrated' and 'child centred' families (Harris, 1980). Harris follows Lasch's notion that the individual's public identities have been proletarianized. They both follow the marxist line that the skills of the work force have been expropriated by a capitalist class through the introduction of scientific management techniques. Deprived of their skills, workers are forced to seek a meaningful social identity through the family. This leads to what Harris terms an 'implosion' within the domestic unit. In his later work this is associated with a form of child-centredness. But in an earlier paper, Harris suggested that implosion could lead to a quite different model of domestic relations. Rather than investing all their emotional resources within the family, individuals opt out of

meaningful family interactions and adopt a more negative consumerist approach to the home. Parents, rather than investing all of their energies in their children as a means of compensating for their 'external' alienation, are treating the home more as: 'a unit of consumption, a base to which members return to eat and sleep and watch TV' (Harris, 1977, p. 399).

Family life, rather than complementing the instrumentalism of the public sphere, then, is duplicating on a smaller scale the disintegration that has taken place in the public sphere of work. Now this model of family relations acts as an interesting theoretical counterpart to child-centredness. It also converges with Donzelot's interventionist model of family life which counterpoises the 'rejected' child with the 'over protected' child (1979, pp. 193–194). As I discussed earlier this typology is absent from Harris's later work on the family. Harris leaves us with only one dominant type of family generated by a later form of the capitalist social structure.

11 Parsons takes a characteristically optimistic line here by documenting the replacement of formal powers over children with more informal, culturally given sets of responsibilities. The professionalization of motherhood is the investment of the process of child rearing with a rationality (Parsons and Bales, 1956, p. 26). Parsons seems to be arguing that mothers are no longer helpless victims of biology and nature. For the very notion of socialization means that mothers are involved in a more technical and sophisticated process of decision making at every minutely defined level of child rearing. Mothers are able to rationally assimilate the information they pick up from the outside about how their own children behave. Mothering is thus no longer conflated with nature.

Chapter 2

Schooling, Discipline and Welfare: The Institutional Context

Introduction

The emphasis on 'standards' within the present discourse on education not only signals dissatisfaction with the content of education but also the way teachers present themselves to the pupils. The critique of classroom discipline has its origins in the *Black Papers* where the emphasis was very much on children being 'trained in civilised manners' and where the 'duty [of the teacher] was to direct, not to remain passive and uncommitted to high standards of behaviour and learning' (Cox and Dyson, 1971, p. 21). 'Liberalism', 'welfarism' and 'child-centredness' were all cited as causes of this teaching malaise (*ibid.*, pp. 98–9).

A more recent and even-tempered version of this argument was published by the Department for Education (Alexander, Rose and Woodhead, 1992). Teachers were accused of applying (and in some cases misapplying) child-centred ideas. Teaching became a form of 'applied child development' which detracted from the business of imparting knowledge in a more individualized sense. The prescriptions are clearly laid out. An emphasis on whole class teaching around traditional subjects projects the teacher back into the centre of the class. The teacher, acts as the visible oracle and source of legitimate forms of communication in class. The teacher dominates by initiating everything, and everything is connected to the intellectual advancement of the pupil. In this situation, teachers are in the best position to assert themselves in checking pupils who get out of hand. Discipline, thus, becomes the public imposition of a set of behavioural guidelines which function both to manage the present teaching situation and shape future notions of public propriety and 'citizenship'.

In one important sense, whether or not there is any truth in the claim that teachers play a much weaker controlling function in class is irrelevant. For the radical overhaul of the content of education – the introduction of the National Curriculum and Standard Assessment Tasks (SATs) – forces teachers back into the traditional mould.[1] The sheer scale of introducing a standardized curriculum, sustained through systematic and periodic assessments, gives teachers little opportunity to 'indulge' in more liberal teaching practices (Brehoney, 1990).

Yet, the crucial link between the impositional nature of these standards and the voluntaristic emphasis on parental choice is the populist notion that parents, if given the choice, would advocate a return to traditional teaching methods (Adam Smith

Institute, 1985). Now recent research (West and Varlaam, 1991) appears to support the contention that 'good discipline' is one of the most important criteria drawn on by parents in choosing a school for their children, but we cannot automatically take this as a critique of existing practice in school.

Assessing the quality of present-day teaching approaches is not the purpose of this study. But we can interpret the significance of school discipline following Wolpe (1988, p. 19), in the way that the disciplinary system in school is seen as the fulcrum for the successful organization of day-to-day classroom activities.

In this chapter I take the proponents of traditional discipline to task on two other grounds. Firstly, that they rely on inferences from theoretical considerations over the education system. To put it simply, according to this thesis, the system is welfarist and the professional ethos is child–centred, therefore teachers adopt teaching styles that are consistent with these tendencies. This overly deterministic approach neglects the effect that the school itself has on the character of teaching. The tension between the standardizing effects of the National Curriculum and the individualizing thrust of school management generates interesting questions about the status of the individual school (Hargreaves and Reynolds, 1990; Hardy and Vieler-Porter, 1990). But the construction of new types of schools will arise out of a combination of legal and political forces imposed on schools from the outside and pre-existing localized differences which depend more on the individual reputations of the schools themselves. We, therefore, have to account for the impact of the school ethos on the running of the school and the organization of classroom activities. This is discussed in the first part of this chapter where I introduce the schools.[2]

A second point of departure from the traditional line on discipline rests on my argument that if the school takes more responsibility for the welfare of the child, then it is inevitable that teachers become more than just 'a controlling power upon (the) will and appetites' of children (Boyson, 1973, p. 138). It does not follow from this that teachers have abdicated their pedagogic duties in favour of a more surrogate parental role. In the second part of this chapter I outline a more positive, disciplinary role for the teachers through the development of a welfare network in school. This includes an outline of the links that the school has with outside agencies, the way that the pastoral system and disciplinary framework feed off each other in producing a network of knowledge and communication and the potential this has for extending the school's influence into the local community.

Finally, despite the constraining effects of policy, social structure and to a certain extent the school ethos on the individual teacher, we cannot predict with any certainty how a teacher will behave in a class when confronted by thirty adolescent students. The third part of the chapter is taken up with an analysis of actual teaching practice taken from teachers' accounts of their disciplinary practices in class. This can be presented as empirical variety which challenges any generalized notion that teachers have lost their disciplinary powers. But at this level of analysis we also identify the creative possibilities for classroom control; possibilities that only arise out of teachers adapting to contingencies; possibilities that are normally translated into teaching routines (Hargreaves, 1979). Although teachers refer to ideas, policies and structures outside of their immediate control, there is still a strong sense of relative autonomy in the way that they manage the classroom situation.

Discipline and the School Ethos

What teachers think and do with respect to the 'consumers of education' and their pedagogic responsibilities is inevitably influenced by the school environment. The individualizing tendencies of the education market place – the introduction of league tables – cannot completely negate pre-existing localized 'reputational' differences that characterize schools. These are made up of underlying sets of norms, values and practices associated with what we might term a school's ethos.[3]

In this section I want to introduce the different characters of the schools with reference to their disciplinary approaches. Modes of discipline and control are key themes in this book. They were also useful subjects through which teachers were able to discuss the ethos of their schools. But in case I contrive a collective opinion from the teaching staff about the unique character of their schools, in the following I distil from the teaching interviews features that make up the ethos of the school and present, where relevant, conflicting accounts of the ethos from different teachers within the same school. In most instances this does not necessarily produce a fragmented image of the schools. As I will demonstrate, differences of opinion normally revolve around the extent to which teachers think their schools live up to their reputations.

Broadly speaking, when asked what they thought their school stood for, five of the eight teachers at St Mary's and Waterston spontaneously mentioned 'standards of behaviour', 'top–down discipline' and 'firmness'. Teachers from Boreston and Stenhouse, on the other hand, emphasized a more cooperative model of teacher–pupil relations. Four of the eight teachers spontaneously mentioned 'pupil-centredness', not being 'authoritarian', and 'negotiating' with the pupils as ways of describing a collective teaching approach.[4] I was not able to assemble a picture of the fifth school, Logan High, from what the teachers said. I briefly refer to what seemed to be relevant to that school at the end of this section.

St Mary's Catholic School[5]

Given that there are few Catholic schools in Scotland, St Mary's is situated in the middle of a much wider catchment area than the average Scottish school; a catchment area that stretches across the northern and western boundaries of the city and takes in a commuter belt of small rural towns and villages. Although its 612 pupils are predominantly Roman Catholic, over the past few years St Mary's has attracted a minority of non-Catholics. There were mixed feelings about this. Some teachers saw this popularity as a consequence of the school's ethos; a 'firm but fair' approach to discipline underpinned by a strong communitarian Christian sense of purpose. Others linked the school's popularity to the new educational reforms. The assistant head when referring to the new reforms argued that:

opting out would be disastrous for us. It would encourage more non-denominational parents to send their children here.

For Bill Short, an assistant head with twenty-eight years' experience at St Mary's, taking the school out of local authority control was tantamount to allowing local parents from all denominations a dictatorial influence that would dilute the school's unique Catholic character. Mary James expressed the same concern over the loss of Christian purpose but referred to this as a product of internal change.

> I'm a firm believer in discipline and there are other staff who are, but there's a feeling that we don't all agree with what comes from the top. I feel that, not from our deputy who's very strong on discipline, but the head's a bit lax here. You know, very much for the kids and falls over backwards to accommodate the kids at times which I feel is not good.

Waterston High School

Waterston High was the largest school with 1141 pupils. Situated on the outskirts of the eastern city boundary in a residential area with a predominantly middle-class population, the staff prided themselves on being able to produce high academic achievers. Waterston thrived on its reputation for being located, according to Liz Sim, in 'an area where parents have very high expectations'.

The teachers were presaging, possibly in an unconscious sense, the pressures that 'magnet' schools are now under to maintain their 'market positions'. Because it was one of six 'magnet' schools within the city, in both educational and disciplinary senses the school had a reputation to live up to. This was expressed by one teacher in terms of the social class backgrounds of the pupils.

> The school is not poor in the things that really matter because the kids are interested in their work, they take a pride in their work and it is of a high quality. It's a school where there is very little deprivation in terms of money. People are basically well off. There are children away from school just now skiing – it's a well-known hobby here, so is golf. The sorts of things that indicate that they have money. . . . The children pay a great deal of attention to where they book their holidays, their parents' type of car, designer brands, things like this.

In one sense, the size of the school shaped a positive image that teachers had of the school in relation to how they felt they were perceived by parents as teachers in what Wexler called 'the pursuit of professional excellence' (1992, p. 72). In another sense, this 'success' worked against any strong collective feelings that the teachers had about the school. Vivien Willis puts the point well.

> In a big school it's difficult to have a cohesive ethos because of the fragmentation by each year head having their own little area of responsibility.

Each in their own way is strict and lets the kids know what is expected of them. In fact, as a cohesive unit it doesn't always come across as one voice. That's to do with size and the fragmentation of the building. There isn't a central area where the school can meet.

Stenhouse Academy

Stenhouse Academy, situated in a small town approximately forty kilometres east of the city centre, has 400 pupils with a guidance staff of six. Over the past fifteen years, with the closure of the mines and a major car manufacturing plant, the area has been marked by severe industrial and demographic decline. Jean Bryce predictably confirmed that a high proportion of this population were working-class pupils at the poorer end of the socio-economic spectrum.

Stenhouse is a poor area. The rector read out some document that said we were the most deprived area in the region outside the city. We have a lot of one parent families, separated families.

As a centre for Orange Lodge activities, Stenhouse is also an area known for its religious sectarianism.[6]

Although in cultural terms Stenhouse was quite unlike Waterston, there was an important similarity in the way that the staff from both schools tended to express the school ethos in terms of parental expectations. But, whereas for Waterston teachers tended to emphasize the supportive nature of the catchment area, at Stenhouse the ethos was asserted in contradistinction to the way parents expected the school to behave. Parental expectations here were linked more to how teachers ought to discipline their children.

The focal point for this tension at Stenhouse was the headteacher who had just arrived from another tough school within the region. He had an almost evangelical approach to changing attitudes both in and out of school. During our first discussion the head took out a belt from his drawer and stated, 'I sometimes produce this piece of leather in class and refer to it as an antique!' The belt symbolized for him the negative, repressive image of the school that he had actively been trying to change as a teacher and headteacher. The belt also symbolized the predominant disciplinary approaches of the parents from within the catchment area when he claimed that many children took an 'awful beating from their parents'. Corporal punishment was seen by the parents as the only answer to the problems of indiscipline in and out of school. According to the head, his views on discipline were very much at odds with those of the parents. He argued that:

disciplinary problems can be minimized by treating the pupil as a motivated individual with his own particular social goals. Teaching has to be directed towards the individual's own ability.

The pupils were to be encouraged to work through syllabuses that reflected a multi-level approach. Thus blackboard-oriented approaches were dropped in favour of what Denscombe has called a 'classwork management approach' (1985, pp. 121–35). The head's argument here was that children were less likely to misbehave if they were kept interested in a syllabus that reflected their own independent needs.

Teaching behaviour in this school was seen in terms of Green and Sharps' (1975) managerial approach, with teachers moving between different groups of children who were involved in tasks that were more suited to their levels of ability. Like the school that Green and Sharp studied, Stenhouse had a reputation for taking in 'difficult' pupils.[7] A child-centred approach in class was seen as more appropriate where children were less likely to accept more conventional teaching methods. According to the head, this teaching approach would further the educational ends of the school, which were about making education more relevant to a mixed ability school. Discipline for the head, then, was not seen as an end product to be associated with its successful exercise by one powerful individual, but an inherent part of the teaching process. Furthermore, although Stenhouse has its fair share of problem children, and despite the exigencies of the education market place, the guidance staff prided themselves on not continually excluding difficult pupils. This fed into the reputation the school had in the wider educational community for being able to deal with children that other schools had discarded.

There was some confirmation of this position from the Stenhouse staff. Ruth Smith, who had been at the school for nineteen years was asked about the school ethos:

MW: I got the impression from the head that this probably wasn't the approach expected from the parents.

RS: Possibly not. But you've got to get through the day; you've got to survive.

MW: Are you told by the parents to belt them?

RS: Yes they often say that. We'll say that we can't. They'll say, 'I don't care just do it'. That's how they deal with it. They tend to beat them about the head. I don't think that's particularly helpful. I'd say 70–80 per cent of staff are child-centred. You can be firm at the same time. The kids don't run amok but we take into account the difficulties the kids have and try to deal with individual kids with problems in an individual way in as much as we can when dealing with groups of kids.

MW: What role does discipline play?

RS: It's important. But at the end of the day the child comes first.

MW: You see discipline as more positive than negative?

RS: Yes, I think so. One or two older members of staff are hard liners. It's very difficult to have one set of rules for wee Jimmy because he's got problems and another set for the rest of the class. I suppose the kids are very understanding.

If we turn to one of her colleagues, Ian Hart, a relative newcomer to teaching, the same views were expressed over the role of the teacher in class but in the form of a critique of the school.

IH: I would say that they [the teachers] all sound to me as if they are teacher-centred. Whereas I see myself as being pupil-centred.

MW: How do you see discipline in this context?

IH: I'm already aware that inconsistencies can puzzle the kids. If they come in from one class where they've had an authoritarian teacher and they come into my class . . . They don't get to do what they want, but I am there to help them. I don't know if they adjust to the change and then going in the opposite direction to another class maybe causes them problems. But I have to say that I'm going to stick with my methods because I'm getting results and no one can dispute that. The kids are absorbing the knowledge. They are learning in a way in which they are retaining. They're enjoying it and they're learning. One or two of the teachers aren't very happy. I've only been here a short time and I think I'm the first person who's gone for this pupil-centred approach. They may feel it's undermining the way they are working.

Boreston Community School

Boreston, a small school with 443 pupils and a guidance staff of four, is situated close to the city centre within a large catchment area. The social class composition is mixed but slightly skewed towards the working class. Seventeen per cent of the school population is of Asian descent. It has strong links with the local community, being a busy night class centre and meeting place for a variety of community groups. It has also attempted to integrate some adults with the children in day-time classes.

The staff interviewed tended to emphasize the same collective approach to teaching and discipline as Stenhouse without parents' expectations as such a potent frame of reference. The spirit of the school is well captured by Joan Leslie, a teacher with fifteen years' experience.

The school should be a caring community. There is the hidden curriculum and extra-curricular part of the school is very important for that. For example, giving all S1 kids [children in first year of secondary school] residential experience together outside of the school. But there is pressure against that from within the curriculum; the parts of the curriculum, particularly new areas, that have been imposed from outside. There is conflict between the declared ethos and pressures from outside. The commitment to anti-racism – multi-culturalism. An essential point to the school is to represent society as multi-cultural and value other races and beliefs – education against racism – that has a high profile. It's for me a very vibrant part of the school because it isn't something that comes from management. It comes more from the staff who are consistently and persistently trying to develop anti-racist education. There is also a gender working group promoting awareness of gender issues. There is also an input from the traditionalists and sometimes there is conflict. The school has been under pressure to close because of falling rolls. It is under pressure to produce exam results. There is a healthy reaction to that in that it has a community school ethos. It's open to adults and has facilities for small kids, the play-group. The school is treating the kids as responsible beings which has been aided by having adults around some in classes. . . . One of the good ways of getting contact with parents is having adults in school. They get a flavour of the school, what a modern school is like. They know everybody, that's a good thing.

Here we can identify a fairly complex set of conflicts between the school ethos and outside pressure exerted on the curriculum, and between progressive and traditional elements within the school. According to Joan Leslie, the formal status of the school as a community school made it much more open to parents. This made it much easier for the school to set itself up as an important source of support to be drawn on by parents.

Although there tended to be a mix between a liberal head and a traditional deputy the emphasis was more on the liberal elements at Boreston. This was expressed by Susan Bruce, who had described her previous school as 'authoritarian':

The pupil is someone to be encouraged . . . own feelings, beliefs, opinions. We should tap into that rather than imposing something else on top. Things like behaviour and progress are things that should be open to negotiation rather than a dictatorial approach. That's the nub of Boreston.

Like Stenhouse there was a similar sense of purpose among the guidance staff, but like Stenhouse there was no unanimity over the commitment of the school to these aims. One member of the guidance team, Jim Craig was much less certain about the school's caring and liberal approach. Jim Craig was a relative newcomer to the school having spent ten years working in a community school with a radical orientation on the outskirts of town. Although his own approach was very child-centred, he was still to be convinced that this was the general approach at Boreston:

157,363

It projects itself as a caring environment but I have to say I haven't really noticed it. As individuals, the staff will say they're caring etc. Their day to day approach to the youngsters . . . they are not very warm, not hostile, but not very warm.

Logan High School

The first four schools can be defined, roughly speaking, according to whether they had more traditional or child-centred approaches to discipline. The staff at Logan school were less able to identify a school ethos. It was similar in social geography to Stenhouse with a predominantly working-class population but was situated well within the city's western boundary. Logan had a serious problem of recruitment, the school having been run down over the past ten years from its capacity of 1000 pupils to the present figure of approximately 460. Like Boreston and Stenhouse, the school had been under threat of closure for several years. The staff referred particularly to the way that the 1981 Parents' Charter had lengthened the waiting lists at the five or six 'magnet' schools at the expense of their own school rolls. The problem appeared to be more serious at Logan with two teachers referring to how this had produced 'low morale' among the staff.

The School as a Welfare Network

The existence of an educational welfare network suggests a series of institutional links between the school and outside welfare agencies. Given the present context of concern over child protection and delinquency we cannot underestimate the importance of these links. I discuss them briefly at the beginning of this section and refer the reader to more detailed expositions of school–agency links (Johnson *et al.*, 1980; Clarke, 1986; Maher, 1987; Carlen, Gleeson and Wardhaugh, 1992). But I wish to remain largely within the perimeters of the school and concentrate on the routine aspects of teaching which incorporate what Finch (1986) terms a 'care and control' element. Teaching interpretations of 'care and control' are discussed later in the section and form the basis of the analysis of parent–teacher relations in the following chapter.

Initially, I am setting out a welfare network as a system of social and emotional support provided for and formalized within the schools. I am thinking principally of the guidance system which functions alongside a system of sanctions that link the school 'management' to the 'front line' teacher. What I set out in the following, is a model of the school's structure drawn from documentary evidence and interview material from the five schools studied. Bearing in mind the differences in ethos between the schools, where appropriate I refer to variations between this model and the particular schools. With the exception of the Catholic school, where the guidance system revolves around a coordinating chaplain, the schools more or less approximate to the following model of a welfare network.

Links between guidance and educational welfare and psychology have been routinized through formal and informal meetings in school which take place at least once a week. With the exception of one or two teachers, the educational psychologist and education welfare officers were seen as integral parts of the schooling system as teachers sought to deal with pupils with a range of social, emotional and learning difficulties. Teaching opinion over these links ranged from the enthusiastic ('very valuable meetings') to the welcoming ('we share the load') and pragmatic ('the psychologist is a resource and I'll tap whatever resource is available').

For the most part contacts with the more 'policing' agencies such as the social services and the police were occasional, largely restricted to serious cases. Interestingly, Craigmount, the one 'magnet' school in the study, was in the process of regulating links with the police and social services through a youth strategy; a multi-agency approach set up to deal with the problem of 'children at risk'. Whereas at Stenhouse where teachers were dealing with far more serious social problems, there was a weaker relationship with external agencies such as educational psychology because of 'lack of resources'.

Internal Network

What is more apparent about the school's welfare function is the existence of an internal and quite complex flow of information between teaching staff with varied sets of teaching and 'welfare' responsibilities. This tends to revolve around the discipline system in school, located at the interface of a hierarchy which separates school management from front line teachers, and a guidance structure which acts as both an early warning system and post hoc source of information. On the one hand, there is a management hierarchy which is referred to in terms of the increasing level of seriousness of the offence committed by the pupil. At a certain point discipline becomes a purely formal process which involves management taking decisions on the educational future of the pupil. On the other hand, there are lesser sanctions which front line teachers administer. First, there are those sanctions that teachers deploy daily in keeping the class under control. These include the use of body language, the raising of the voice, and the moving of pupils to other parts of the classroom. Although these sanctions were set out in the school handbooks and parent guides, the circumstances within which teachers invoked them were not dictated by school policy. Further up the disciplinary hierarchy, sanctions increase in severity and seriousness and, importantly, involve an external referent. These sanctions are more formalized in the sense that they are usually recorded and involve a third party, either a member of the management team, the guidance teacher or the parent. The key ones are listed below:

Punishment exercises: Either lines or essays on topics chosen by the teacher. These have to be signed by at least one parent.

Detention (after school):   Keeping children within school outside of normal school hours. These have to be recorded and the parents informed.[8]

Behaviour forms: Children are given forms which have to be signed by the teacher after every class with a brief remark on behaviour. They also have to be signed by at least one parent. They are then reviewed after a designated period of time.

Withdrawal from the classroom: Invoked normally where classroom behaviour has reached crisis point. A referral is made to the principal teacher and the year head. The pupil is normally sent to the Unit, variously known as the 'referral centre', the 'sinbin' and the 'cooler' for a predesignated period of time.[9]

The most serious sanctions are those that involve an enforced absence from school. First, school management can exclude pupils from school for a limited period through temporary suspensions. Secondly, there are permanent exclusions. This is a hotly contested issue at the moment and I will have more to say on this subject in the final chapter. But at the time of the research, the decision to exclude a child was still taken by the regional director in conjunction with advice from the teaching staff involved.

When discussing exclusions the teachers were all able to produce exceptional circumstances where the offending pupil had committed such a serious infraction of the school's rules that the pupil was excluded without reference to any previous past record of misdemeanours. But in the main, the use of exclusions followed a predictable path of misbehaviour met by incrementally more serious sanctions. These sanctions were invoked because the school was able to produce compelling evidence over a lengthy period of time that the pupil had a history of problems in class. As one teacher remarked:

If the pupil has got to the stage of suspension or exclusion . . . we have had a lot of contact with that pupil and parents. We would have a fairly comprehensive picture of that pupil.

One crucial factor here is the existence of a guidance system which supplemented and to a certain extent underpinned the system of sanctions. Guidance was made up of promoted teachers whose teaching time is split between their pastoral responsibilities and their subject timetable.[10] They are responsible to a junior member of the management team, usually an assistant head. Guidance teachers will receive referrals from heads of departments and principal teachers. These will have originally come from front line teachers. These referrals are formal pieces of information on a pupil who is giving some cause for concern.

For example, one of the perennial problems that the teachers have is pupils who persistently do not do their homework. They have exhausted the level of sanctions that subject teachers are able to invoke on their own, and are referred upwards to their principal teacher and outwards towards guidance. Information flows upwards from the subject teacher as sanctions increase in severity, and information flows sideways as the guidance system is alerted to potentially serious disciplinary problems.

The Early Warning System

The early warning system cropped up time and time again in the teachers' accounts of their guidance responsibilities. The teachers were clearly aware of the need for formal recognition of a child's problem from other teachers before taking further action. But the notion of teachers being able to detect problem children very early on served to emphasize the informal and 'pre-formal' characteristics of the school. The former refers to an ongoing network of informal links that run parallel to the formal flow of information within the school. The latter refers to the early stages of 'problem formation' before the pupil's behaviour is recorded in any significant sense.

First, teachers, especially the more experienced, were able to detect problematic symptoms in the first few weeks of a child's secondary school career:

> In S1 [year one of secondary school] after ten weeks we'll circulate views from teachers on the kids, a settling-in report. Even at that stage the sore thumbs will be showing.

Experience, according to Ruth Smith from Stenhouse, is combined with the character and size of the school.

> A lot of the information I get tends to be informal. Once you've been in a job for a long time you can spot them from day one virtually. Because the school is small and many of the teachers have been here for a long time, and because there are very good informal ties between the staff, we tend to have good communication and know how the kids are behaving and become aware of a problem at an early stage.

Where teachers do start to report on these pupils, guidance will still try to keep the problem at the pre-formal stage by feeding into the informal reservoir of teacher talk in the staff room. Susan Bruce had responsibility for the younger pupils and tended to bring up the subject of problem pupils casually in conversation:

> S1 are just beginning to find their feet as certain characters are emerging. I tend to if I get a few bad reports on that pupil I'll say to other teachers, 'by the way so and so is causing a few problems'.

Whether we are talking about a formal or informal early warning system, guidance, in the institutional sense, can be seen as a system for detecting problematic symptoms early on and building up case histories of problem pupils (Best and

Decker, 1985). Teachers are able to draw on wider and more detailed versions of the child's moral, social and educational development. Provisionally we might say that a framework has been provided that gives teachers a great deal of 'policing' potential. Rather than produce a simple pedagogic summary of the child, the guidance teacher is able to construct a detailed case history of the child's social development.[11]

If we acknowledge the sequential development of 'problems' in school, the home is inevitably drawn on by guidance. In the following chapter I discuss the cultural limits to a more complete enclosure of the family within this network. But it is worth mentioning at this stage that the pre-formal and informal aspects of the network were often discussed by the teachers in the interviews as a way of emphasizing their ability to contain problems within an educational context. The early warning system could be invoked as a means of alerting others to potential problems in school. But teachers were reticent at this stage to involve parents. Dorothy Small provides an illustration of this point.

> DS: In the early warning system I would have the child in to discuss the situation, and quite often this chat is enough initially.
>
> MW: Do you contact the parents through the early warning system?
>
> DS: Not necessarily. At that point the teacher just wants us to be alerted. It may be that after several early warnings that I would say, 'now we've talked about this, you've been give a punishment exercise and you're back here again. It really would be unfair to your parents not to let them know how you are doing.

Disciplinary Troubleshooters

Guidance extends even further; it goes into the realm of desires and anxieties of children. First, guidance teachers took responsibility for the non-examinable aspects of the curriculum, such as personal and social education, which included sex education. (I will discuss this further in Chapters 5 and 6.) Guidance teachers also took great pains to stress the importance of their 'confessional' role in providing a private space for adolescent problem solving. As one teacher stated:

> Getting to know the children, for a guidance teacher that's paramount. To get the kids to talk to you; to tell me their problems at home and at school. They come to me as an outsider before they want to go to their parents, either because they think it'll upset them or they're scared of the parents.

Now this was not simply a way of asserting a non-interventionist means of moral influence over the child – even though teachers favoured 'educational' solutions to the problem of 'inadequate parental socialization' (see Chapter 3). Teachers here were keen to emphasize a therapeutic mode as a way of asserting the non-disciplinary nature of their guidance responsibilities.

I have discussed the way that the guidance system underpins the framework of sanctions in school. Where children were causing teachers some concern, guidance teachers were usually informed and asked to play a role. For some guidance teachers this was a perennial source of difficulty and confusion. From their own vantage points as classroom teachers, discipline was an aspect of their teaching approach they were acutely aware of. As I will go on to demonstrate later in this chapter, classroom control was an important precondition of teaching. All teachers were expected to be disciplinarians in this respect. But the guidance teacher's perception was that where a subject teacher wasn't able to handle the classroom situation, and where a child's behaviour warranted inclusion within the formal disciplinary system, the school would look to guidance for the answers. Guidance teachers within the schools were being seen as disciplinary troubleshooters. According to Bill Smart, this put them in a negative light in relation to the pupils:

> Generally, my role is a go-between supporting the pupil. I don't see myself as the disciplinarian – that's the AHT's [assistant headteacher's] job. Discipline is a dodgy area I always felt. I see myself as responsible for discipline in my house (as a house master) and as a teacher in general. In terms of suspending or excluding kids I see myself as making a case for the child. Sometimes it's a hopeless task. I'll be there with the AHT and the parents and the child saying that he has this or that problem and that perhaps to exclude would be a bad thing . . . at the end of the day I see myself as the provider of information for these pupils.

Bill Smart saw himself more as an advocate of the child in circumstances where the child needed support in presenting a case against possible suspension or exclusion.

Other teachers like Jean Bryce were happy to stress the surveillance aspects of their role, where children who seemed to be causing some concern could be given support. But this support was supposed to connote the care and attention sometimes required from guidance rather than the negative associations often made by her colleagues between guidance and sanctioning:[12]

> It's going to be very difficult, but I am working with a nice wee girl who doesn't cause any trouble in class. Some folk think it's only the trouble makers that occupy our time, but this little girl is pleasant, chatty. But she's beginning to keep the wrong company. She's also a bit flattered by the attention of the boys who are looking at her for the first time. We'll have to spend a lot of time and care on her, I think.

Guidance teachers here were echoing the distinction made between 'welfare' and 'discipline' in the Elton Report (D.E.S. 1989: 114). Teachers who had a tendency to draw on the guidance system as soon as there was a problem in class were less likely to be good disciplinarians, teachers with good 'group management skills' (ibid. p. 69). Yet, there is no tension here between welfare and discipline. The Elton Report stresses the importance of a pastoral network as an educational safety net which teachers are expected to draw on for two reasons; as a last resort after classroom techniques of control have been exhausted, and as a means of detecting early signs of a deviant 'career'. Guidance teachers were also keen to strike a balance between providing a 'background' to an indisciplined pupil and working through adolescent traumas with individual pupils. The pastoral system in school, rather than replacing the more informal and individualised techniques of control in class, can be seen as a precondition for dealing with a wide range of behavioural, emotional and social problems in class.

This is an important point of departure from the educational critique discussed in Chapter 1. For the suggestion here is that taking a welfarist approach to problems in school necessarily dilutes classroom discipline. Discipline and control in class in these terms are narrowly defined in terms of the 'positional' difference between teacher and pupil (Bernstein, 1971).

According to Bernstein, the educational structure not only creates a welfare network within school, but undermines the individual teacher's capacity to exercise an educational authority in class. As teachers focus on educational failure and indiscipline in class, in terms of the social and emotional backgrounds of the pupils, they become less concerned with asserting their authority in class. Teachers present themselves in Riesman's (1950) guise of the 'compere' who provides merely the broad parameters within which pupils work at their own pace within the group.

The organization of classwork has changed in response to the new educational values. Group work is argued to encourage cooperative rather than individualistic efforts from pupils. Within this context teachers find it difficult to take the kind of immediate action in class argued to be necessary in establishing and maintaining control. Two points are worth making here. First, this argument suggests that the positional difference between teacher and pupil alters as the teacher works through a group of pupils instead of demanding the undivided attention of the whole class. The work of Sharp and Green (1975) has shown that discipline and control take more subtle hidden forms when teachers use group work. Indeed, establishing classroom control through group work may produce a different kind of moral pupil – the cooperative rather than competitive child. But it does not follow that children are any less subject to the influence of the teacher.[13] In the following analysis I argue that a 'managerial' approach, rather than being a deviation from a traditional norm, is an alternative approach to discipline and control in class.

A second point relates to how and when teachers might take on a more managerial role in class. The recent critique of a loss of control in schools focuses on the way that schools since Plowden have uncritically adopted a series of fashionable teaching approaches. Clearly, the daily requirements of the curriculum, the level of the children being taught and the potentially heterogeneous nature of the pupils' characters means that teachers selectively draw on the appropriate features of any teaching philosophy where and when relevant. In the following I identify a few teachers who see their teaching style as part of a professed teaching ideology. In the interviews I asked teachers to identify the core features of their teaching styles and their associated beliefs. I have organized these beliefs in terms of general categories of teaching laid down by the critics of 'schooling and welfare'. Yet, within these broad categories I have also discussed the ways that the exigencies of teaching dictate a more adaptive approach to any teaching philosophy or belief system.

Classroom Discipline

Autonomy and Classroom Practice

In this section I address classroom practice more directly by treating the class-room as a 'micro-culture' (Vásquez and Martínez, 1992). That is, the assumption made here about the nature of teachers' work is that the quality of action between teachers and pupils cannot simply be determined from either the moral or organ-izational character of the school or, more broadly speaking, the structure of the education system. Despite the well-defined location of the individual teacher within the teaching system, the majority of teachers asserted a degree of autonomy within the classroom.

One of the key themes running through this book is the extent to which the idea of the family as a private sphere is compromised by the 'socializing' activities of others. Yet, the same sense of separation from the outside as a means of more personal and internal control could be detected from what teachers said about their professional identities. For Liz Sim from Waterston High, the classroom was a pri-vate professional space:

> Teaching is a very private thing. You're in your own classroom and although your head of department will put his head in, or should put his head in, you're virtually unsupervised.

I hinted earlier at teacher autonomy when discussing the way that teachers were expected to deal with discipline problems in class in the first instance in their own terms rather than drawing on guidance. Teachers were very conscious of the extent to which they referred pupils to those outside their immediate teaching locus.[14] A few teachers were quite happy to ensure that the school management was aware of the steps they were taking as regards to certain pupils. Ross Stewart saw this as an important way of safeguarding his position from potential negative reactions to his teaching:

> Some teachers run their own personalized detentions. I tend not to. I like the management of the school to be aware of what's going on within the school. Lots of teachers have their own modes of discipline. Quite often it never comes out in the wash . . . Although I don't over indulge in it, when there's something specific, I'll put it down on paper. I want the management to know what I'm doing. Most of the time most of the teachers will deal with things themselves.

Yet the general issue here is the assertion of classroom responsibility as a form of professional autonomy. I referred earlier to the 'sin bin' as a means of dealing with breakdowns in class. Teachers tended to think that removing a child from class could have a damaging effect on a teacher's competence. One school, Boreston, had a much more liberal policy here in allowing teachers to use the full range of sanctions available. Susan Bruce compared the sanctions used at Boreston with those used at other schools:

> I'd use the unit for dealing with really troublesome kids. It's not seen as a big deal here. It's not an admission of defeat on the part of the teacher. In another school you would have been interrogated as to why this pupil was out of your class.

Teachers in the other schools would occasionally refer to informal versions of the 'sin bin', usually in terms of how the constant need to be seen to be supervising a problem child limited the extent to which they were able to place the child 'out of sight'. Some teachers were able to improvise:

> They'll get a punishment exercise, that's basically it. Any more problems and I'll put them outside the class. This isn't a good thing because they are unsupervised. In my [biology] lab there's a wee room and I put them in there sometimes and they can do their work there. (Norah Bowles)

Teachers were conscious about drawing on external support in dealing with classroom indiscipline because it reflected badly on their ability to teach, not simply how they were judged by other teachers, but how they were seen by the pupils. When asked whether he tended to hand out punishment exercises in class Ian Hart replied:

> I did fall in to that trap when I started teaching. It's a sign of failure to do that. That in itself opens up new avenues and new possibilities for the teacher to demonstrate his incompetence . . . it's public in front of the class when a kid's given a P.E. [punishment exercise]. If that kid refuses to do that P.E. that does far more damage to that teacher's credibility than if they had not given the P.E. and just shrugged his shoulders.

Similarly from Anne Smart:

> I very rarely ever use the early warning system, apart from children doing the 'O' grade course who haven't done their homework. I think I'd rather sort this out without drawing on other teachers. I think the children think all the better of you if you sort it out yourself.

The responsibilities placed on teachers to keep order within the classroom tended to put them in a unique position in finding solutions to the perennial problem of keeping the class interested and well behaved. Despite some of the rationales offered by the teachers as a form of democracy within class, all teachers were in the business of setting the classroom agenda. All teachers were thus in the business of asserting a control over affairs within class. Contrary to recent criticisms of schooling which conflate 'disorder' in class with progressive teaching philosophies, I follow Denscombe (1985, pp. 143–6) in arguing that quite disparate teaching styles can be seen as different techniques of control.

Denscombe identified three approaches to classroom control adopted by teachers; domination, cooptation and classwork management. Domination approximates to the conventional teaching approach of 'chalk and talk' (Hammersley, 1990, p. 54). It also comes close to the notion of teacher sovereignty proposed as the only acceptable form of teaching by the critics of welfare. The emphasis is placed on status, respect and deference; in Denscombe's words 'a public display of the hierarchical relationship which obtains between teacher and pupil' (1985, p. 99). The other two approaches, on the other hand, emphasized the downplaying of the teacher's 'public' authority, whereby the status of the teacher is underplayed in an attempt to win over the confidence of the pupils. Cooptation places more emphasis on pupil participation in the organization of the classroom agenda, and the use of reason in trying to restrict misbehaviour in class. Classwork management places a greater emphasis on the teacher, using such factors as classroom space, the curriculum and the variable quality in educational attainment levels of the pupils in 'managing' classroom behaviour.

Very few of my teaching respondents fitted the categories exactly and there was considerable overlap between domination and classwork management, and between classwork management and cooptation. The former overlap has more to do with the changes in curriculum and more general changes in teaching. But there is still a sense in which the differences are great enough between domination and classwork management approaches to warrant separate categories. The overlap is too great between the cooptation and classwork management approaches with my sample. I have, thus, brought both categories together under the title of 'cooptation as classwork management'.

Dominance

Thirteen of the teachers saw the external imposition of forms of behaviour as an integral part of their teaching responsibilities. 'Discipline' was something that was exercised from the 'top down'. Sometimes this meant the head setting an example. More often than not it was left to teachers to impose their authority within the classroom situation. Yet, although there were general similarities in terms of an emphasis on a public display of dominance in class, there were significant differences in how teachers asserted this dominance. It became apparent through the interviews with these teachers that, although they were articulating their approaches in terms of how they were able to impose their status on classroom proceedings, this tended to take several different forms. I have, therefore, broken down this group into three sub-types which reflect the different verbal approaches teachers used in asserting their authority in class.

Six teachers argued that they had to constantly assert an authority through their superior verbal skills. These teachers relied more on a *confrontational* approach. These are teachers who see verbal confrontation as part and parcel of their disciplinary roles. Bill Smart from Waterston saw the raising of his voice in class as an important visible expression of his authority. In these terms the social and intellectual powers of the teacher are manifest in an attempt to maintain the upper hand in a situation where the teacher is heavily outnumbered by the pupils. Bill Short from St Mary's would often give his pupils a 'quick blast of the voice' when his back was turned or when he had to leave the room and returned to find that his pupils had moved seats. For one of his colleagues, Ian Dury, there was almost an expression of sheer enjoyment in verbal confrontation:

> [He] invariably ended up in an eyeball-to-eyeball confrontation . . . kids like confrontation, adults don't. Most adults will back off from confrontation, I won't. I'll have a confrontation any day of the week. I'm certainly not going to be dictated to by small kids.

A second group of four teachers adopted a more *psychological* approach in consciously trying to refrain from 'bawling out' their pupils. This was taken as the major motivating force in maintaining control. Whereas in the previous example the teacher saw the successful control of the classroom in terms of how he would verbally square up to a badly behaved pupil, teachers who favoured this alternative approach saw this as a sign of failure. There was, thus, a concerted effort made in avoiding confrontation. Ross Stewart from Logan High argued that the worst thing to do is to have a confrontation with badly behaved children because adults will always come off worst in these situations:

> I feel a lot of kids like the conflict situation and if they can see that the teacher has had to raise his voice then, although they're getting a row, its still one up for them because they've managed to niggle the teacher.

Here we can see the classroom as a battle of wits. Not being drawn into confrontation on which the pupil thrives might lead to more effective control. The emphasis is placed more on the teacher asserting an authority through the displaying of greater psychological skills. This is brought out in Ross Stewart's approach to disruption in class where he will:

> try to maintain a normal level of conversation. Quite often the more serious it is the quieter I'll speak and the closer I'll bring the kid to me.

According to Ross Stewart the type of pupils who engage in this kind of exercise are the type of pupils who have nothing to lose in taking the confrontation 'all the way'.[15]

Finally, a variant on the both the confrontational and psychological approaches was the *economic* use of the raised voice. Three teachers were able to avoid confrontation by only occasionally resorting to the raised voice. This was more of a considered economic act in that, as Vivien Willis from Waterston stated, 'if you were always shouting . . . it would lose its effectiveness'. Its effectiveness was measured in terms of the immediacy of response from the pupils. Vivien Willis described one of the few occasions she raised her voice:

> There's always noise [in class] but to me the noise level was unacceptable. I said that we'd have to keep the noise level down or those responsible would be punished. A few minutes later somebody started arguing with someone else over a pencil sharpener and I gave that boy a punishment. At the end he came out and said, 'Miss, I've never had a punishment in class. Nobody has had a punishment in maths. Do you think I'm really bad?' He was really worried. The effect on the others was amazing.

Teachers here raised their voices sparingly when there was a need to restore order. They tended to adopt a firmer approach at the beginning of the session in an attempt at establishing ground rules for behaviour in class. Vivien Willis started out with a new class by being:

> particularly firm. Strict but fair I would hope. You can always slacken off later. Mostly my classes develop into being fairly relaxed. You set out guidelines fairly clearly and people know what's expected of them.

These teachers would tend to associate the confrontationalist approach with a never ending and inefficient use of a teacher's limited resources, where a teacher is never able to slacken-off.

There is a strong overlap between the psychological and economic approaches in that, through experience, teachers dealing with large classes of restless pupils couldn't hope to compete by using verbal force alone. Confrontation reflected badly on teachers and prevented them from being able to teach effectively. Most of these teachers were in the business of preventing situations ever getting out of hand. Thus, there was a big emphasis on the introduction of a code of conduct, if you like, a classroom ethos, in the first few weeks of term. This was not necessarily related to externally defined sets of standards – the teachers were not simply in the business of 'socialization' – more the acknowledgement of the difficulties encountered through teaching without any practicable guidelines (Docking, 1980, pp. 12–39).

Coopting the Pupils and Classwork Management

A dominant approach in class suggests that 'action' emanates from the teacher with pupils appearing to passively respond to the teacher's initiatives. Teachers adopt a range of verbal techniques for maintaining this position in situations where action originates from outside the teacher's locus of authority. Pupils' 'initiatives' are by and large rendered illegitimate through these techniques. If we turn to an alternative approach to classroom discipline in class, seven of the teachers, rather than abdicating any responsibility for keeping order in class, underplayed their authority by adopting what Donzelot termed a 'relational' approach with the pupils (1979, p. 211). Six of the seven teachers were from Boreston and Stenhouse with professed child–centred approaches. The teachers here emphasized the *cooptive* aspects in their work which involved a degree of responsiveness to the initiatives from the pupils. Their strategies relied on trying to form relationships with the pupils on a much more equal footing as a way of coopting their attention in class. On several occasions Jim Craig from Boreston tried to underplay his formal authority. He asserted:

> I don't operate as if I'm God, you know, I'm up front and you guys have to jump through my hoops.

Ian Hart from Stenhouse asserted a more cooptive approach in opposition to what the pupils were used to. In the process, he referred to the idea that a particular teaching approach might have to accommodate the age of the pupils.

> Older kids I try to relate to more as adults and equals. The young kids are still looking for a domination type of situation, a benevolent dictator. They're quite disappointed if they don't get it.

Neither teacher was able to avoid a degree of boundary setting. In fact there was no sense in which any of the teachers in the study were expressing the more radical views associated with schools like Summerhill (Neill, 1962). Almost all teachers saw themselves taking full responsibility for setting the agenda in class over what was acceptable behaviour. Jim Craig mentioned a degree of collective respons-ibility within the classroom:

> I tend to place the onus on shared responsibility between myself and the youngster. We're equal partners. What I will be doing will be picking up people for lateness. I tend to throw that back on to the class. The class will be in agreement that being late to the extreme is unacceptable, is disruptive to the whole class. Not just something that bugs me, it bugs everybody.

Yet, it was left to Jim Craig to define what was to count as an issue that would affirm the collective ethos.

Two other teachers who rejected a dominant role in class favoured a *class-work management* approach which incorporated a cooptive element. These teachers underplayed their formal authority and controlled the class through managing the parts of the curriculum that the teacher was able to set in class. Joan Leslie and Susan Bruce from Boreston incorporated aspects of classroom management into their approach. Joan Leslie structured the pupils' behaviour in class because she normally had a degree of autonomy over the content of classwork. She then used the lesson as a way of involving the children in activities in class thereby minimizing the possibility of pupil disruption.

> My long-term approach is to have a relationship with pupils so that I minimize the formal and semi-formal sanctions unless the pupil is very disturbed. Once I know the pupil I don't tend to have to use sanctions. However with this particular group I'm doing a syllabus that I feel is not very exciting and interesting. I don't have very much control over it . . . tend to have to be a bit heavier than normal . . . involves not allowing kids to sit together . . . I prefer to get them to work in groups.

In situations where she had less control over the curriculum some degree of 'dominance' was necessary.

Susan Bruce used a form of group management in organizing any classwork that involved a high degree of noise, traditionally a sign that a teacher had lost control of the class (Denscombe, 1984, pp. 230–56).

> I wouldn't say they [the pupils] saw me as a stern disciplinarian. On the other hand, there's not much mucking about. However, someone who likes to impose authority in the classroom probably sees my room as rather noisy. So, on the whole, they respond pretty well because of the friendly atmosphere.

Noise was for her a sign that the class was behaving properly in that her pupils were more involved in classroom activities. I went on to ask her more specifically about the kinds of informal sanctions she used.

> I always work with the children in groups so I would be asking is it threatening the work of the others in the group. That's my first criterion. If it is I would split the group up and the badly behaved child might be taken out.

Corporal Punishment and Classroom Autonomy

In the earlier discussion of the discipline system, I set out a hierarchy of sanctions that ranged from personal and informal modes to more formal and externally determined procedures. Teachers asserted their classroom autonomy by stressing the personal and informal resources that they drew on in keeping control. I have argued that in their guidance capacity the teachers here were advancing this position as a way of keeping 'discipline' separate from 'welfare'. As classroom teachers they were also attesting to the importance of 'self' control as part of a professional teaching ethic. If we turn briefly to the thorny issue of corporal punishment, the assertion of classroom autonomy can be read into teaching opinion over the banning of the

Table 2.1:   *Teaching views on corporal punishment (N = 2.0)*

Group A: Those in favour of its return	7

Bill Short	– 'cure 75 per cent of unruly behaviour in the classroom'
Ian Dury	– 'sometimes need to be cruel to be kind'
Mary James	– 'an important means of establishing discipline'
Jean Bryce	– 'an important weapon in establishing authority in the first couple of weeks of a new class'
Vivien Willis	– 'useful in certain situations, for example, bullying'
Ross Stewart	– 'performance of school would greatly improve with its reintroduction . . . other sanctions not as effective'
George Barry	– 'more effective sanction than anything they have now'

Group B: Those unequivocally opposed	8

Ruth Smith	– 'obviated bureaucracy . . . wasn't effective . . . didn't like giving the belt'
Ian Hart	– 'doesn't want results through fear and oppression'
Ian Howe	– 'indication of failure on the part of the teacher'
Bill Smart	– 'vicious . . . hypocritical . . . too often abused'
Jim Craig	– 'totally opposed, personally and professionally'
Susan Bruce	– 'hated it on principle and any practical benefits'
Joan Leslie	– 'hangover from Calvinism'
Anne Smart	– 'opposed to whole idea of legitimate violence'

Group C: Opposed, but recognized a degree of effectiveness	5

Ian Jones	– 'I'm opposed . . . a recent convert to the cause . . . if used sparingly was effective but I don't think it's right to inflict pain on kids'
Norah Bowles	– 'I want something as effective as the belt but not the belt itself . . . opposed to physical violence as any mother would be'
Liz Sim	– 'never liked using it but it had some deterrent value'
Alice Tay	– 'in principle not necessarily against . . . only a few kids might benefit . . . quite often abused'
Dorothy Small	– 'ambivalent . . . quite an effective deterrent but I don't think its reintroduction would make society a more disciplined place . . . bit hypocritical belting somebody for fighting'

belt.[16] A second more general point can also be made about classroom sanctions if we assess the views of all teachers on corporal punishment.

Although recent debates have focused on legislative attempts to abolish corporal punishment in the independent sector, the spectre of the old traditionalist position within state schools has appeared in recent Government pronouncements over the 'Back to Basics' campaign (Ward, 1994; Preston, 1994). Strands of the opposing liberal position are prominent in the accounts of classroom sanctions from the teachers opposed to corporal punishment. Table 2.1 illustrates the philosophical and moral arguments. I also referred earlier in the chapter to the way that the absence of force as a sanction within the school was used by some schools, notably Stenhouse, to differentiate the socializing role of the school from the socializing roles of parents within the local community.

Without establishing any necessary relationship, we can link the different disciplinary styles to groups A and B shown in Table 2.1. All advocates of corporal punishment (or the belt) took a dominant line in class whilst all coopting teachers were totally opposed to the belt. But if we group together the teachers who advocated the return of corporal punishment (group A) with those who were against the belt in principle but claimed it had a practical and deterrent use (group C), we can detect an implicit critique of existing sanctions and arguably the suggestion of a loss of disciplinary autonomy in class. Teachers nearly always referred to their own personal verbal and psychological resources when discussing their informal sanctions in class, but where teachers found it necessary to take more serious action, the need for an 'immediate' sanction, the demand for a more 'effective deterrent' in class and the desire to 'avoid bureaucracy' were recurring themes. Those who advocated the return of corporal punishment tended to see the belt as a necessary, if not central, means for both establishing and maintaining authority in class. If you like, it acted as a symbolic marker for drawing the teacher's locus of autonomy in class.

The abolition (or should it be 'the return') of corporal punishment also highlights the relationship between individual approaches to discipline and the school ethos. First of all, I compare responses from traditional and child-centred schools, St Mary's and Boreston, respectively. Teachers were asked what they thought about the banning of the belt.

St Mary's

In favour of its return:

Bill Short – 'cure 75 per cent of unruly behaviour in the classroom'
Ian Dury – 'sometimes need to be cruel to be kind'
Mary James – 'an important means of establishing discipline'

Opposed, but recognized a degree of effectiveness:

Ian Jones – 'I'm opposed . . . a recent convert to the cause . . . if used sparingly was effective, but I don't think it's right to inflict pain on kids'

Boreston

Unequivocally opposed:

Jim Craig – 'totally opposed, personally and professionally'
Susan Bruce – 'hated it on principle and any practical benefits'
Joan Leslie – 'hangover from Calvinism' (all cooptive or classroom management)

Opposed, but recognized a degree of effectiveness:

Alice Tay – 'in principle not necessarily against . . . only a few kids might benefit . . . quite often abused'

All four teachers at St Mary's, then, believed in a 'top–down' disciplinary approach at school and classroom levels. All four teachers were implicitly critical of the way that the loss of the belt had robbed them of an effective means of establishing and maintaining their sovereignty in class. Although Ian Jones had become a 'recent convert to the cause', he still emphasized the need for an immediate sanction that teachers could draw on in asserting their authority.

Boreston, on the other hand, was much more interested in establishing itself as a community centre through its sensitivity to cultural difference. I discussed this earlier in the chapter, but it is worth reiterating this point because the school, in one sense, exhibited the idea of leadership through the head teacher's influential position within the community. In another sense, any hierarchical difference between the school and the working-class community, and teacher and pupil was less marked where the emphasis was both on building up relations with parents across a range of different cultural and socio-economic groups and the lessening of 'generational' differences as the school actively encouraged pupils from all age groups. The key word is cooperation and this underpinned the pervasive belief in child- or student-centredness in the school. It also informed the individual teacher's approach to classroom discipline in class. It was no surprise, then, to find that the guidance staff were opposed to corporal punishment in school.

Conclusion

Classroom autonomy was a key theme running through the teachers' accounts of how they approached discipline and control in class. We might be forgiven for thinking that if these accounts had been produced in the mid-1990s, discussions of classroom autonomy may have sounded like a lament for a golden pre-National Curriculum past. It is interesting to note, for instance, that one teacher had to adjust her cooptive style 'upwards' where she had less control over the curriculum.[17] Nevertheless, we cannot be certain that teachers have significantly less control now than they might have had in the late 1980s. In this chapter I have followed Andy Hargreaves' notion that although policy frames and delimits what teachers do in class, it cannot completely determine the ways that they control the classroom situation.

I have argued that the welfare network in school incorporates an important disciplinary axis from which guidance teachers gain more insight into the range of problems that are identified in class. Yet, from a teaching point of view this did not necessarily lead to a softening of their disciplinary positions. A majority of teachers claimed that their disciplinary approaches were still dictated by a need to assert their authority on classroom proceedings. Furthermore, 'softness' of approach cannot be simply read as a loss of control in class. I have not simply demonstrated that 'chalk and talk' in its various guises still governs the way teachers perform in class. Personal preference, backed by a compatible set of school values shaped for some teachers more sophisticated and hidden forms of classroom control.

What these different approaches collectively demonstrate is the commitment to a particular form of order in class. Without understating the importance of their pastoral roles, there was still a tendency to think that curricular matters took precedence over pastoral responsibilities (Power, 1991). The teachers in this study, at one level, were asserting a professional ethos which privileges the teachers' class-room autonomy over demands made on them by the school organization. Yet, teachers emphasized two facets of their guidance positions that compromised this perception. First, discipline was a formal precondition of guidance, in that guidance positions were promoted posts and 'good discipline' was taken as an important criteria for promotion. Second, the development of a welfare network in schools had the effect of both formalizing and extending the knowledge that teachers had of school activities, pupil behaviour and social background. Teachers might suggest that this knowledge was accrued over time – 'naturally' – through an informal network of teacher talk. But, guidance played a strategic role in linking discipline to school management and the school to the local community.

A final localized factor, the school ethos, conditions this assessment and underpins the disciplinary approaches of the teachers. The professed teaching philosophy of the school, the perceptions of the school vis-à-vis, first of all, the parents and, secondly, the education community, and an understanding of what Carlen *et al.* (1992) called the social geography of the school, underpinned the teachers individual belief systems to varying degrees. Sharp and Green (1975, p. 47), when discussing the influence of the school, argue against the 'reification' of the school ethos as a set of principles upon which the school was organized. As I have shown, teachers from the same school did not always express the same views about what their school stood for. Nevertheless, most of the teachers were able to express a collective sense of their school's position on discipline. With reference to classroom teaching practice, it was easier for teachers to practice their own professed teaching approaches if they were congruent with the ethos of the school.

The reader might be forgiven for thinking that teachers are hardly likely to admit to disorder in their classrooms given the importance they placed on keeping order in class as an aspect of their professionalism. Yet this would assume that any misbehaviour in class is a direct result of something that the teacher has or has not done. In Chapter 1 I outlined the importance of an agenda that asserts the role played by parents in shaping their children's behaviour outside of the home. We need not then assume that teachers are bound not to admit to problems they face in class when they are perfectly capable of pointing to children as products of someone else's work. Disciplinary problems that teachers have can often be identified in terms of the quality of parenting. Arguably, these assessments are made much easier given that the school as a welfare network opens up possibilities for more 'relational' links between teachers and parents. It is to these perceptions that I turn to in the following chapter.

Notes

1 Soon to be replaced by 'level indicators'.
2 The teaching sample can be found in Appendix 1.
3 For a more detailed discussion see Wyness (1995, forthcoming).
4 See Reynolds and Sullivans' study of eight schools which compares 'coercive' and

'incorporative' strategies as ways of characterizing control in schools (Reynolds and Sullivan, 1979).

5   I changed the names of all respondents and schools. I have also significantly altered the geographical setting of the schools whilst maintaining an accurate, although admittedly impressionistic, description of the social characteristics of the areas in which the schools are situated.

6   The Orange Lodge is a semi-clandestine male only organization of a sectarian nature. The membership is avowedly Unionist, the 'Orange' referring to the succession of the protestant William of Orange to the throne in the seventeenth century.

7   Some teachers commented on how the Parents' Charter of 1981 had led to many parents within the area sending their children to schools with better reputations. This didn't radically effect Stenhouse's intake because the school often took in pupils who had been excluded from other schools.

8   This can be differentiated from the more informal variety where detention is imposed by the classroom teacher during the lunch break.

9   For an extended discussion of the functions of units, see Tattum in Ribbins, 1985, pp. 43–6.

10   See Appendix 1 for more detail.

11   See the discussion of 'risk profiles' in the Elton Report (DES, 1989, p. 116).

12   In Chapter 4 I discuss the strategies that parents adopt for keeping tabs on children who are being led astray. Jean Bryce clearly demonstrates the same kinds of anxieties felt by parents where a pupil is being picked up through the early warning system.

13   Hammersley (1990, p. 54) makes the same point when addressing the way that teachers tend to refer to teaching approaches other than their own in terms of disorder in class.

14   A point made by Denscombe (1984) in his delineation of the more informal processes of control within schools. See also Tattum in Ribbins (1985, p. 51).

15   *c.f.* Willis's 'lads' who at the level of the school had transcended the exchange of deference for the teacher's knowledge (1977, pp. 52–88).

16   The schools involved in the study had all, in varying degrees, followed an informal policy of banning corporal punishment before it was made illegal in 1987. See also Wolpe's (1988, p. 273f) summary of the debates over corporal punishment in schools and research carried out by Cummings *et al.* (1981) in Scotland.

17   Recent analyses of teacher cultures focus on the heightened importance of collaboration and cooperation as a consequence of curricular change (A. Hargreaves, 1994, pp. 187–212; D. Hargreaves, 1994).

Chapter 3

Parental Primacy and the 'Best Interests of the Child'

Introduction

The previous chapter alluded to the limitations of inferring teachers' actions from the formal and theoretical requirements of the school. Although there maybe a general shift towards assessing problem pupils, with respect to their social and emotional backgrounds rather than their cognitive and intellectual abilities, this did not appear to inhibit the pedagogic roles of teachers in class.

These limitations are more clearly identified when trying to match the potential of the school for policing parents with the accounts that both parents and teachers give of where responsibility lies for the moral and social welfare of children. Any notion that teachers can dictate the responsibilities parents have for the discipline of their children, or in some cases take over the parental role, needs to be set against the assumptions made about the respective spheres of influence of parents and teachers. These assumptions, or lay social theories, are examined in the first part of this chapter from both a parental and teaching perspective.

The second part of this chapter deals with how guidance mediates between the home and the school. Given the generally expressed notion that parents take responsibility for the discipline of their children within the private sphere of the home, and given also the institutional and professional imperatives of acting in the best interests of the child, the guidance role is fraught with difficulties where actions need to be taken in response to a perceived break down of parent–child relations. Although the current agenda focuses on alleged incursions by state agencies within the family, any discussion of a home–school division of responsibility logically refers to limits imposed on parents encroaching upon the educational responsibilities of teachers.

Although teachers tend to refer to problem parents in terms of more conventional notions of social deprivation, I argue that the guidance system in school generates an alternative model of problem parents which derives from the experience teachers have of parents who implicitly question their educational expertise. Part two, then, examines how encounters with parents generate quite different models of problem parents which reflect common-sense notions of intervention by both parents and teachers.

The Limitations of Discipline and Surrogacy

The Parental Perspective on Primacy

Many of the parents implicitly drew on Riesman's (1950) notion of the psychological gyroscope in summing up the difference between the role of the school and the role of the family. What comes through generally from the interviews is that parents come first, in the obvious biological sense, but they are also seen as primary in guiding their children out into a world outside of the family. We can say here, then, that parents have *primacy* in the sense that they are the figures who have most influence over the cultural development of children. The setting of the moral and cultural homing device (a not accidental metaphor) is symbolized by the notion that parents 'bring up' their children. Parents tend to dominate in the early formative years of the child before the school plays a part.

Nowadays, this temporal division between school and home has been muddied by the tendency of parents to send their children to either nursery or play group. This is borne out by the parenting sample. Only one couple interviewed had not sent their children to nursery. In theory, 'schooling' – the first formal contacts their children had with the outside world – started as early as the age of three for some parents. Nevertheless, we cannot simply see this as the school encroaching upon the time that parents previously had with their children at home. Parents articulated important differences between school and nursery in that there was no compulsion to send children to nurseries. Despite the fact that educational reform throughout the eighties has been underpinned by the theme of 'parental choice', parents asserted important differences between the compulsory nature of schooling and the optional nature of the nursery.[1] More importantly, there was also a sense for the parents that, compared to the school, the nursery was seen as a way of gently introducing the child to the outside world, rather than having any intrinsic educational purpose.

Table 3.1 shows that of those parents who gave a reason for sending their children to nursery, a majority saw it as either an accepted part of bringing up their children or as a means by which their children were able to mix with children of their own age before they went to school. There was little sense, then, that parents expected their children to be 'educated' at nursery. The nursery had more to do with parents introducing their children to the social world, a responsibility that was part of the more general parenting idea of 'bringing up' their children. What parents appear to be saying here is that the school has lost a social function of being the institutional locus through which children are introduced to their peers. This would appear to strengthen the idea that the school was primarily the means by which children are 'educated'.

'Bringing them up' is not an easy phrase to neatly encapsulate for it seems to cover everything from the amorphous emotional investments that parents make to the more rigorous exercise of discipline through the setting of standards. Discipline, though, is something that the school takes some responsibility for according to one parent, Richard Stone.

Table 3.1: *Why parents sent their children to nursery/playgroup (N = 25)*

Reasons given by parents	Nos of parents
A parental norm	10
The need to mix with other children	11
Necessity (both spouses working)	2
Giving mother more time	1
Getting mother out of the house	1
Total	25

The school has to discipline them. They've got them for the day. It's up to them but if somethin' happened and he came home, I'd go up to the school to find out what had happened.

Yet, some parents offered a different emphasis. Jan Short argued that the family and classroom settings are not equivalent. Teachers are dealing with different problems in class because they are dealing with groups of children. Thus, the school in terms of discipline is not simply capitalizing on the good work of the ideal parent: once a child enters the classroom, behaviour is guided by quite different criteria. There is no necessary direct reproduction of the child's misbehaviour at home in class. The way that children respond to their parents maybe qualitatively distinct from their behaviour in school. This point was expressed by Jan Short.

Sometimes parents look at things in a different way from the teachers. Parents have the one child, whereas teachers have all these others to deal with.

It might follow from this that the responsibility a teacher has for disciplining the child cannot be referred back to the inadequate socializing of the parent. That is, if the child behaves badly in school it is because of factors which the parent has little control over, given that the classroom is a different setting. Interestingly, this point is not pursued by Jan Short because she continues in the vein of the other respondents who saw a direct relationship between parental inadequacy and problems in school, in particular, the difficulties the school encounters when parents try and pass on the blame for their own inadequacies as parents.

Quite often the parents think they know more than the teachers about the school and they can blame the teachers for their problems . . . You do have to know what your child is up to, even though they're at school all day, within reason. To me, kids play a lot more truanting nowadays because the parents don't know about it or don't want to know about it. They tend to blame the school; it's their fault. Once their child is out the front door it's the school's responsibility. Then where does it start or stop. I would say you can't take your child to school for ever – they get older and want to go themselves . . . there are parents who go out to work who don't have a clue what their child does. It must be worrying, so they've got to blame someone and I think that's more or less what they're doing. It's very hard to say it's my fault for her being the way she is. But it's got to come from the home. If your kid is swearing and cursing they're hearing it from somewhere. They hear it at school but if they are in the habit of hearing it [i.e., in the home] then it's just like a second word to them.

It is here that the idea of parental responsibility for discipline is most strongly expressed. Parents may be making a perfectly rational claim in blaming the school, given that their are qualitative differences between relations in the classroom and relations at home. Yet, ultimately, responsibility for parents is not about the apparent rationality of a situation. Responsibility here is a question of making judgments over who came first and who has primacy.

Unwanted Advice

The idea of responsibility was unequivocally expressed by parents in discussions over the rights that others had to offer them advice on how to discipline their children. The parents were almost unanimous in asserting that other authority figures had no right to offer them advice on how to discipline their children. One working-class father, Dave Deary, had a strong sense of boundary between 'family' and the outside world. He was asked about how he and his wife disciplined their children.

We give them a right ticking off. Getting back to the way I was brought up. That's the way I try to bring my children up. If you start to teach them right from wrong to begin with.

He then offered an unsolicited critique of the social services.

I'm a total disbeliever in social workers. Only once have I ever had contact with a social worker . . . Billy (his 15-year-old son) had been off school for quite a long time with a broken arm. A social worker appeared and really upset the wife. It was just lucky I was home from my work that day. The way they carried on. I put her out of the house and told her 'no social worker will ever be back here' . . . My mother and father were my social workers.

Social workers, not unexpectedly, are clearly designated as interlopers here because they were seen to unconditionally supplant the parental role. The idea of intervention is strengthened further as George Deary elides a physical notion with a cultural notion of intrusion. The social worker's physical presence within the home reinforces the threat to the parents' sense of authority within the family (Allan, 1989; David *et al.*, 1993).

If we turn to the input from teachers we might have expected a different response. As I mentioned in the introductory chapter there is a widely held belief that teachers have an important disciplinary role in school. Furthermore, teachers may not be felt to have such an intrusive physical presence within the home. We might speculate that any teaching intervention would be related to more distant cultural notions of 'influence' or unwarranted and unsolicited suggestions dropped casually into conversations at parents' evenings. Yet, parents were equally hostile to any interference from the school.

Parental primacy was just as forcefully and unequivocally expressed in discussions over the rights teachers had to offer them advice on how to discipline their children. If disciplinary boundaries were not always clearly demarcated by parents with respect to a division of responsibility, the parents were unanimous in asserting that the teacher had no right to offer them advice on how to discipline their children. One father, Bill Wilkins, was asked whether teachers had ever tried to advise him on disciplining his sons.

> I think one or two of them. The maths teacher tried to tell us how to deal with him [his eldest son]. I just looked at him like, and said I'll bring up ma' weans [children] ma' way.

Many more parents expressed resentment that any teacher would dare to offer advice. The Slaneys were unequivocal in their rejection of any attempt by teachers to influence the way they brought up their children. Agnes Slaney responded by drawing on the parent–teacher division of responsibility.

> *MW:* Do the teachers ever advise you on discipline?
>
> *AS:* No. I don't know if I'd take too kindly to that. I wouldn't dream of telling the teacher how to educate them so I wouldn't like them to tell me how to bring them up.

Discipline, according to her husband, a company director, was something that took place within the home because parents had to install the 'moral gyroscope' before children started school.

> *MW:* Do teachers ever offer you advice?
>
> *BS:* No. I wouldn't take any either. I have strong views on that. I've always been strong in that respect. I believe at an early age they should know what's right and what's wrong.

Teachers' Assumptions and the 'Best Interests of the Child'

Parental primacy over discipline was articulated by teachers when addressing the responsibilities they had towards children vis-à-vis parents. But teachers tended to offer a different approach to these responsibilities. The teachers, when asked about their relationship with parents, stressed the importance of working together in the interests of the child. For many teachers this meant that parents and teachers had to complement each other.

> Idealistically, there should be a complementary relationship. What they're hearing at school should be backed up with what they are hearing in the home about the socialization process. (Susan Bruce)

At this abstract level various general aims and ideas are incorporated. The best interests of the child sometimes meant ensuring clear lines of communication between parent and teacher in situations where the child is able to exploit the spatial difference between the home and the school.

> I think that any cooperation between parents and teachers is bound to be beneficial. We've got the same aims to do what is best for the kids. Sometimes children imagine that parents and teachers can't communicate. They also try and play off teachers with parents. They'll pretend that their mother doesn't understand what I've said. When you talk to the parent you often find that it's a ploy. (Vivien Willis)

In the previous chapter I suggested that teachers had different approaches to the task of setting an agenda in class. At the more abstract level of serving the best interests of the child there was a general consensus among teachers that this would be best served by improving the lines of communication between parent and teacher. Parents and teachers were both seen as agents of socialization here in that the socialization of the child can only be successful if there is a level of consistency between what parents and teachers do. Socialization, then, also incorporates the notion that there is a certain equality of responsibility between parents and teachers. Alice Tay stated:

> I wouldn't set myself up against the parent. Although you do come up against parents who hassle you, you have to divorce yourself from it. I don't set myself up as an expert. I don't set myself up as someone who is more informed than the parent or more qualified in dealing with their kids.

At such a high level of generality, working together implied that parents and teachers each have a legitimate power over children. But in specifying the sources of these powers, that is, defining the areas of responsibility that teachers and parents have, there is the introduction of important differences. Whereas, the teacher has certain moral and social as well as educational responsibilities, the parents' responsibilities are bounded by biology, nature and early affectivity. When asked to compare the rights of parents with the rights of teachers, Dorothy Small stated that:

> Our rights are . . . the old phrase in *loco parentis* of course, but however much in *loco parentis* you think you are, you are still dealing with a group

of pupils who are, I hesitate to use the word, strangers, about whom you've got to objectively say, 'Why are these pupils here?' These pupils are here because I want to teach them history, I want to teach them how to be good citizens. I want to teach them how to get on socially with each other . . . Hopefully you like all your pupils, although it's not always possible and you don't let them see that you don't like them if you're a good teacher. But they are, as it were, separate from you. Whereas, a parent who has brought a child into the world is bringing that child up in that family unit; has a much closer tie and has a much nearer contact . . . is not looking at the child so objectively . . . is legally responsible for the child until the age of sixteen or eighteen.

Reference to the position of the teacher in '*loco parentis*' is interesting. Writers of a marxist persuasion (Shaw, 1981; Fitz, 1981) take the interventionist line in suggesting that this is an ideological device for underwriting a range of interventions within the family. But what was being expressed by this teacher was the limited and temporary nature of a teacher's powers in relation to the child.

The expression of these powers by guidance teachers served to highlight the primacy of the parents' responsibilities. According to the teachers, parents are supposed to dominate in the early formative years of the child before the school plays a part. For the school this could mean, as is quoted in an important study of teaching practice, that parents produce 'school trained children' (Sharp and Green, 1975, p. 86). The emphasis in Sharp and Green's study appeared to be on the role parents played in making children more manageable for teachers.

In this study the guidance teachers had a more global view of the impact of parenting on the child. Early parental investment was crucial not just in relation to the underwriting of harmonious teacher–pupil relations, but was important in the production of socially competent members of society. The teachers here invoked a boundary between school and home drawn on by critics of the welfare state in terms of the different responsibilities that parents and teachers had. In an important sense, the teacher's separateness from the parent was heightened by the knowledge and experience of parents with whom they came into contact. This paradox informed most of their dealings with parents.

Ross Stewart illustrated this point when discussing the difficulties of maintaining the boundary between the parents' and the teacher's responsibilities.

The teacher deals with industry and the future. Specific areas they're asking for children to be trained in specific skills. The teacher comes in and does a professional role. Everyone has to work. Full-time education is a vital necessity. That's our role in life and it allows the parents to be fully involved in their lines of work because they need to earn a living to maintain standards. So the role of the teacher is important but I think the role of many teachers is extended. Some teachers are the only contacts the children have. Some teachers are the only representation of discipline that kids have.

This is the conventional notion of the teacher as instrumental provider of skills which historically replaced the educational functions of the parent (Parsons and Bales, 1955). This version of parent–teacher relations also comes closest to the parental notion of primacy. This version, though, is an idealized version of what the parents who were interviewed took for granted. Ultimately, from the teaching perspective, this is the point where any imputed responsibilities that parents have come into conflict with the experience of trying to maintain these disciplinary boundaries. Ross Stewart very clearly identifies the expansion of this educative role to include the moral work which ought to have been already undertaken by parents. According to some teachers, parents are not doing enough parenting because the teacher is forced to take on more of the parental role. This point was reinforced by Anne Smart, a colleague of Ross Stewart's:

> One of my feelings is that parents don't do enough with their kids and tend to say to us I don't know what to do with them. They look to us to help them out. Parents don't play as big a role as they should do in bringing their children up and looking after their interests at school. We do extra because of the lacking of many families. In many ways parents perhaps expect too much of us. They seem very helpless. They see the school, not only in its role of educating the kids, but hopefully they look to us to help them sort it out because they cannot sort of come to any solution to the child's problem. They tend to come up to the school and ask for our help. Very often we have put parents in touch with social workers and other agencies. I think we're very valuable in that sense. I don't think that many parents would know what to do if they couldn't come up to us.

Lay Theories of Problem Parents

I have argued that a paradoxical situation arises where teachers' views on parents' responsibilities are expressed in a way that parents are seen to have abdicated these responsibilities. Unlike social work, where professionals are in a direct sense concerned with the influence that parents have over their children, guidance teachers pick up on parental influence as a consequence of problems defined within an educational context. As I argued in the introductory chapter, the current social agenda defines the 'best interests of the child' as a rationale for unwarranted intrusion within the private sphere of the family. Yet, where 'intervention' takes place in school there is a different kind of tension between the responsibilities of parents and the responsibilities of teachers. The behaviour which draws the guidance teachers' attention in classroom situations is defined by teachers as a problem which has its origins within the home. This was clearly stated by Ian Jones.

> I know this is a cliche but it's not the kids. Nine times out of ten it's the parents who are unsettled and not disciplining their kids properly. There are no bad kids, maybe one or two, but you can imagine if dad's in the

pub every night or mum's on her own with four or five kids or she's maybe out working at night, the whole thing unsettles kids. A good stable family background with good support from mum and dad and you rarely get problem kids. They may not be bright and intelligent but you won't get the trouble. If you dig into the background of the ten to a dozen kids who are a problem in the school it's all family. There's always something in the family.

Earlier I discussed how parents failed to differentiate between social workers and teachers where their parental authority as disciplinarians came under threat. From the teachers' perspectives this difference seemed to count. Where the professional *raison d'être* revolves around the moral and physical protection of the child which directly focuses on the parental role, those professionals are placed in the firing line where there is a perceived increase in state activity around the perimeters of the family. Teachers can identify the same kinds of familial inadequacies as social workers, but teachers can fall back on the idea that the best interests of the child, at the very least, start with a basic responsibility towards the child's *educational* well-being. In practice, this means that teachers are potentially in a better position to legitimate any intervention by drawing on education criteria. Furthermore, as I will go on to demonstrate in Chapters 5 and 6 on sex education, the moral work of teachers can usually be presented in educational terms. Nevertheless, teachers expressed similar anxieties over intervention within the private sphere of the family.

Guidance teachers tended to see problem pupils in terms of their family backgrounds. Guidance teachers were part of a communication network between the home and the school that was set up to deal with the child whose problems could only be effectively dealt with through the family. Yet, there was some ambivalence expressed over the action that the individual teacher takes to remedy this situation. For, as we have seen, the majority of teachers saw discipline outside of the educational context as an immutable parental responsibility. The teachers had a strong sense of their educational responsibilities and went to great lengths to underplay their role as primary disciplinarians.

I don't tend to point out to parents what they should do. I might ask if their children are very tired in school. I'll mention that and ask what time he goes to his bed. I may make some noises about them coming in earlier. But I don't often say to parents, 'Look, he should only have one pound for pocket money. I don't see it as my role to tell parents the error of their ways. (Norah Bowles)

Teachers who were parents themselves seemed to be more acutely aware of the pitfalls of setting themselves up as experts in child rearing.

I'm the last person to tell parents how to discipline their kids. With certain parents, in discussing their kids, you can point out how things are done in school and enquire as to how things are done at home. As a teacher and a parent myself you've got to be careful about how you approach things. I'm very wary about pointing the finger and accusing them of this or that. I'm interested to get parents and kids to talk about their experiences at home. If handled properly, parents will respond. They'd be the first to tell you to mind your own business if you asked about their sanctioning. (Bill Smart)

Although teachers tended to define children who were a problem in school as products of inadequate parenting, they were wary about attempting to solve the problem through getting involved in family matters. The problem was compounded by parents who solicited help from the guidance staff. Several teachers claimed that some parents saw the guidance teacher in a more positive light as an ultimate sanctuary in situations where parents had lost control of their children. Teachers were well aware that this situation would ultimately force parents into a more dependent relationship with the school which could easily breed parental resentment towards the school. With the guidance teacher as the link between the home and the school, guidance teachers were more acutely aware of how parents might see the school than other teachers. Although guidance teachers wanted to foster relations with parents who were having difficulties, they didn't want parents to become dependent on them.

We're a line of communication between the rest of the school and parents . . . an aid to them in helping them to bring up their children. Helping their children go through education happily . . . I like parents to think that they can use my first name . . . to get away from the idea of me as somebody in authority or an extension of the school management and disciplinary structure. It's important that they don't see us as checking up on them or their kids. We're there as a resource. (Joan Leslie)

These tensions were less apparent in discussions with teachers from St Mary's. Teachers from the Catholic school tended to be more at ease with parents than teachers from the non-denominational schools. The paternalism of the Catholic school through its communal ties with the church made the surrogate parental role much easier to manage. When asked whether parents ever solicited advice on discipline, Ian Dury replied:

All the time. There was a funny situation three years ago with a family in Bilton. They had a little boy, a right little bastard. I'd taken him home one day, father had heart trouble and wasn't able to exert himself. I was sitting on a stool and I said to the father, 'I'd put him across your knee and wallop him.' He said, 'Well, you do it Ian', and the boy was beside me. I said, 'Do you mean like this?' [goes through the motions of spanking the boy]. He said 'Yes, but harder and I give you permission to do that. If you like I'll put it in writing.' I said, 'I don't know if that will be necessary but I promise to do it.' I had no intention of doing it. When I was leaving he gave me the stool I was sitting on and said, 'Take it with you, it's the right height.' He wasn't joking.

It may be that the image of the school as part of the Catholic community in the northern part of the city weakened the boundaries between the home and the school and this had the effect of weakening any notion that the school might, from time to time, have to play an intrusive role. But this still needs to be offset against the common notion among the parents and teachers in this study that the parental responsibilities were scrupulously separate from the school's.

In the previous chapter we discussed the inappropriateness of a more pedagogic approach to teaching at Stenhouse. Teachers acknowledged that many pupils came from deprived backgrounds where they had missed out on crucial levels of parental support. This tended to be reflected in the discussions over the kinds of relationships that they had with parents from the school. Jean Bryce expressed the concern that at his school parents too easily assumed that the school or the social work department would take responsibility for child rearing.

> In this area a lot could be done for us to try and make the parents more aware about what goes on within the school. They don't know what I do as a guidance teacher. We should let the parents know who we are and what we do and also what their responsibilities are . . . They do tend to shunt responsibility to the appropriate department and just leave it there and then criticize the system if there's a failure.

Teachers in these situations may, to all intents and purposes, be acting as surrogate parents. Yet, teachers at Stenhouse were not advocating that they ought to take over from parents. The teachers here were very conscious of what they ought to do in situations where problem pupils were the products of problem parents. Jean Bryce made it very clear that there was a need for the guidance teacher to advise parents more specifically where their responsibilities lay as child rearers.

Finally, there is an interesting contrast between the views of teachers from Stenhouse and the teachers from the community school in Boreston. Both had professed some form of child-centredness. Yet, rather than see the extension of the teaching role as a negative compensatory factor, teachers at Boreston tended to express more positive reasons for acting in *loco parentis*. Within the same abstract framework of 'the interests of the child', guidance teachers from Boreston tended to see their guidance role in two ways: as an important mediate link between the home, the school and the outside world; and as a private forum where children might air personal problems.

> I think it's important that teachers do feel that they are I suppose in *loco parentis*. They need to take on more than just their subject and get involved in outdoor educational visits . . . get to know the kids. For a guidance teacher that's paramount. What is crucial as a guidance teacher is to get the kids to talk to you; to tell me their problems at home and at school. I've

had one or two situations where I've had to broach the problem at home with the parent and persuade the child that they can talk to their parents about it. They come to me as an outsider before they want to go to their parents, either because they think it'll upset them or they're scared of the parents. (Susan Bruce)

The guidance teacher, rather than simply compensating for parental deficiencies, was creating a private space for adolescent problem solving which would facilitate much closer links between parent and child. Although teachers from Boreston and Stenhouse had similar child-centred approaches in class, their guidance roles were dictated by external criteria. Whereas, at Stenhouse, teachers spent more time compensating for earlier parental inadequacies, at Boreston the kinds of pupils they had, the emphasis on opening the school out to the community, and the more mixed catchment area, allowed guidance teachers to spend more time as guidance teachers of pupils rather than parents. We might add that the role of the guidance teacher was much more confidently asserted at Boreston than at Stenhouse because the guidance role was less bound up with the parental role. Finally, we might add that where teachers were able to define their professional role in relation to the pupils rather than the parents, teachers had a much stronger sense of guidance having an educational function.

Social Class

I have already established that much of the guidance teacher's time is taken up with problem children. I have also established that guidance teachers are strategically placed to construct accounts of these pupils which highlighted their social backgrounds. I now turn to the ideas that teachers have about the types of families with which they have most involvement. We need to know more about how the teachers understand these as social problems. One way of doing this is to assess the relative importance of social class as a criterion of evaluation when teachers identify problem behaviour in class. It is plausible to point out that guidance teachers were predominantly involved with children from economically and socially deprived families; parents who had neither the material or intellectual support to offer their children (Carlen *et al.*, 1992, pp. 94–101; Paterson, 1989, p. 46). Table 3.2 provides a rough guide to the significance of social class as an explanatory framework from the impressions that teachers gave in response to the question on class.

From this rough calculation there was a lack of consensus over the impact of the family's socio-economic status on the behaviour of the child in class. The issue was complicated by the two working definitions the teachers had of the problems they most commonly confronted as front line and guidance teachers, namely educational and behavioural problems. Norah Bowles from the poorest school commented on this.

The less able children tend to come from a poorer background because they haven't had the support, or the parents aren't interested in school, or

Table 3.2: *'Do you think social class is important in assessing misbehaviour and indiscipline in school?' (N = 20)*

Teacher response	No. of teachers
Strong social class connection	9
No strong social class connection	11

they don't get support for homework or support enforcing the school's discipline. Many of the badly behaved come from middle-class backgrounds. I think there's a distinction there. The less able kids educationally probably come from poorer backgrounds but badly behaved kids in this school came from middle-class backgrounds: it's across the board.

Teachers can draw on examples of highly motivated middle-class pupils with behavioural problems. Alice Tay who had just moved from a school in an affluent city suburb to the more culturally mixed inner-city community school saw little connection between social class and problem pupils. She was asked about what type of children caused problems in class.

Sometimes it's the brightest kids from the best backgrounds. It's an attitude problem that you wouldn't find in other kids. They can be very superior sort of, 'I don't have to listen to this' . . . Middle-class kids are very confident in their perceptions in how things should be. Often they'll openly criticize teachers. You do get this kind of arrogance which you don't get in a school like this.

This point was also expressed by one of her school colleagues, Susan Bruce. She was asked whether class was an important factor.

I don't think so. It's quite widely spread in this school across different ethnic backgrounds and social backgrounds. One of the most difficult boys is in S4 [year four of secondary school], his father is a Labour Councillor. Although I suppose I do deal with him slightly differently because I see him as a leader. If I can persuade him that an activity is worthwhile he tends to carry a lot of other boys with him.

Susan Bruce here introduced the idea that even if there is little apparent causal connection between misbehaviour and social class, teachers might be expected to respond to a child's misbehaviour in terms of their social class. This can be interpreted as sets of expectations teachers had of how children from particular backgrounds ought to behave. This point was also brought out by Ross Stewart who emphasized the importance of the social geography of the school. At the same time, however, he was also able to point to middle-class 'exceptions' who were able to avoid being labelled as a problem.

I'm generalizing here, but our worst children tend to come from the Silverton area. It's recognized as the poorest district. We seem to get more remedial children from there. Having said that we have one or two pupils. . . . one in particular who comes from a good home who is probably one of the nastiest pieces of work you can imagine. The annoying thing is that pupil is educated and knows exactly what he's up to.

What can be said here is that the models, ideas and preconceptions that guidance teachers had of these problems tended to be defined in terms of particular types of social relations within the family. This was clearly expressed by Ian Jones when asked about whether he saw problem pupils in terms of their social class backgrounds.

It's never in my mind, it's never a consideration. Maybe if I reflected on it by looking at individual pupils but at the time it's irrelevant. It's not social class it's what's happening at home. A rich kid can have just as many hassles if parents are divorced as a poor kid.

Within these considerations guidance teachers undoubtedly came across clearly defined products of socio-economic deprivation. The four guidance teachers from Stenhouse, the school in the poorest area, tended to think there was a link between the poverty in the area and the high numbers of problem pupils in school. Yet, this needs to be set against the idea of there being family types that exist independently of socio-economic factors (Toomey, 1989). Lay social theories on problem children may be shaped by the need to avoid any labelling tendencies in the classroom or, more simply, as a professional reaction to 'classism'. Therefore, we need to be careful when dismissing social class as the basis for the lay theorizing (Wyness, forthcoming). Nevertheless, the quality of relations within the family would appear to structure understandings that teachers had of problem children (Emerson, 1969; Eaton, 1983). The following quote is from a teacher at Logan High, a school where social class conditions ought to dominate the explanations teachers have of problem children.

I would say, rather than coming from certain backgrounds in the social sense, I would say that they came from certain types of parents. You tend to find a pupil who is a barrack room lawyer shouting the odds instead of doing what is required of him. Demanding his rights in the sense, 'Its no' fair'. I would say that the parents are either like that or they're possibly parents who have several children who have not got full control over the situation, where there is a lot of competition at home to be heard. More that kind of thing than social background. I can think of pupils from this kind of parent (the barrack room lawyer) in all kinds of groups, and I can think of the more disruptive kids from families where they've got to compete for attention. Again that can come from varying social classes. (Dorothy Small)

Maternal Irresponsibility?

A second causal factor was linked to gender differences within problem families which converged much more with the notion of the mother being the target of welfare. Walkerdine looks specifically at the way mothers are targeted by teachers in the way that she suggests that the quality of mothering is linked to explanations of deviant children (1990, pp. 36–7). There is some suggestion from the teachers in the present study that problem children could be explained with reference to a maternal irresponsibility. Teachers were asked to comment on which parent responded to punishment exercises handed out to their children at school. Thirteen teachers claimed that mothers sign the forms before they were returned to school. The majority of teachers took this as an indication of a maternal responsibility for discipline within the home. Responses here were compounded by an awareness of children from single parent backgrounds. But mothers seemed to be involved where there was another parent around.

> It's one parent who seems to be in charge of sanctions at home. The other parent's involvement is, 'Oh, that's the wife's job'. Ideally, it would be great if both parents came to the school, but in reality it's just the mother. When we are in contact with the home 90 per cent of the time it is the mother who plays the role of the carer of the child, who comes to school, discusses the discipline and attendance. (Vivien Willis)

Teachers often made judgments about the mother having responsibility. Reference was made to the way children are able to exploit parental difference in terms of one parent being weaker than the other.

> Mothers usually sign but I ask for both signatures so that both parents are aware. Sometimes the children play one off against the other. They'll get the one that they can get round their little finger to sign it. (Anne Smart)

There is some suggestion that problems didn't simply stem from an over reliance on mothers as disciplinary figures. Alan Prout's (1988) work on mothers and their primary school-aged children suggests that one of the ways that teachers judge the competency of mothers was through the mothers' handling of their children's sickness absence from school. We can detect a similar process here but rather than just compare mothers against some standard of maternal normality, mothers were being compared less favourably with their spouses. Some teachers felt that mothers had a weaker disciplinary approach than fathers. Punishment exercises were often accompanied by:

> . . . excuse me notes from mothers. Our kids tend to go for big sisters and grannies as well. All the soft options. (Ross Stewart)

> I would say probably mothers [signed punishment exercises] because they think that mum would be less strong about being upset. Sometimes we insist on the father signing. (Dorothy Small)

Absent Parents

As outlined in Chapter 2, a lot of time is spent by guidance teachers with parents whose children are picked up through the guidance/disciplinary network. Although parents can be alerted to these problems very early on at general parents meetings, teachers tend to involve parents when the child's problems reach a certain degree of seriousness; when several of that child's teachers raise the issue with the guidance teacher. I also referred in the previous chapter to how the early warning mechanism encouraged classroom teachers to contact the guidance/discipline network when a child started to exhibit certain problematic 'symptoms'. The problem can be gently raised at routine annual parents meetings where behaviour can be more discreetly incorporated into general discussions about school performance. From the teachers' point of view these meetings are held every year for all parents, organized by school year. These are formal meetings that teachers expect parents to come to, to discuss their children's progress. These meetings can also be important forums for the discussion of discipline. In practice, discipline merges into other areas of equal importance. But teachers will sometimes need to focus on the behaviour of a particular child when asked about that child's progress by the parent.

> Parents want to know two things: does my child behave in class and how well is he doing in the subject. Most of them ask if their child gets homework, and claim that they never see the child doing enough homework. The main worry seems to be over their child's behaviour. (Anne Smart)

The problem for teachers here is that this process ought to involve all parents in routine low-level interactions with teachers. In practice, however, teachers generally only get to see parents whose children are not causing any great concern. Within these routine contexts teachers never get to see the parents of problem children. Teachers were expressing a commonly felt concern about the kinds of parents who had few contacts with the school (Macbeth, 1984, p. 39). Ian Hart went on to provide an explanation.

> If we could divide kids up into well behaved, normal and badly behaved, it's parents with kids for the first two categories. These parents are not going to receive any flack. The very bad ones stay away. These are the ones who have to be invited in individually. Some parents have been criticized so often by police and social workers they never come to school.

Joan Leslie, from Boreston, made a similar distinction when outlining the problems that some parents faced.

> The ambitious parents come concerned for their kids' futures. The group who it is very difficult to see are the ones whose kids are having problems for reasons that might be related to the home situation; financial pressure,

marital problems, problems with housing; or people who have often had bad experiences themselves and see school as quite an oppressive place.

The teachers were arguing that problem children were a product of some form of parental deprivation. These were seen as obstacles for certain parents, preventing them from taking up the more routine lines of communication with the school. Teachers were then forced to draw on the guidance/discipline network within the school in order to contact these parents. These contacts took the form of either informal phone calls by the guidance teacher or more formal letters.

The schools were very conscious of heightening relations with parents by requesting their attendance in school. Teachers were aware that parents tended to see these requests as implicit criticisms of their disciplinary skills. Teachers often adopted less conventional tactics in trying to avoid the necessity of individual 'consultations'. Boreston had set up a parents' meeting specifically for absent parents with unfortunate unintended consequences.

> You very rarely see the parents you want to see. We had a parents' meeting where teachers were told to invite parents they wanted to see. That was actually quite interesting. A couple of parents came who were very defensive – 'What do you want to see us for?' – I think they abandoned it, because they thought it had generated so much resentment from the parents because they know of parents who hadn't been called in: 'They're not being called in, but I am'. (Alice Tay)

Quite often a phone call or a reply to a letter was sufficient. In some circumstances more drastic measures were adopted in trying to track down parents who apparently didn't want anything to do with the school. Parents were either summoned to the school or home visits were sometimes arranged in an effort to get hold of parents who were unable or unwilling to come into school. Although thirteen of the teachers saw home visits as part of their guidance responsibilities, they were treated with some caution. One school in particular, Stenhouse, which to some extent had set itself up as a social alternative to the home, had no policy on home visits and guidance teachers were quite suspicious when the interviews turned to this subject. Having said this home visits, on the face of it, posed few difficulties for teachers other than the time that they consumed. In circumstances where a parent was unable to get to the school and where the teacher was involved in giving work to pupils with long-term illnesses, the teacher would normally negotiate a mutually convenient time with the parent.

The home visit could be seen as an important means of building up stronger links with the parents and as a way of getting a more accurate picture of the problems the child faces within the home. Yet, there was here the same tension between wanting to get an accurate picture of the problem pupil's home life and the experience of dealing with that pupil's parents. Although teachers thought home visits were a good idea, in practice they often found the experience uncomfortable. Ruth Smith, who adopted a more cooptive approach to the teaching process, recounted the difficulties maintaining her role as a teacher on occasions when the visit was instigated by the parent.

> Not many of us do home visits. On a couple of occasions a parent has asked if I would go to the house and I've done that. On another occasion, when I was trying to speak to another parent whose kid was involved with the youth strategy group and she was finding it difficult to get here, it was just as easy for me to go there. That was very interesting because you don't feel nearly so confident . . . its a totally different situation. You're so used to marching along, 'Come in, Mrs so-and-so'. You're in her territory. It's very, very different.

There is a sense here that the teacher was invading the private territory of the parent. Because the visit did not create any heightened sense of occasion, and because there was little sense that the teacher was questioning the disciplinary or moral responsibilities of the parent, it is the teacher who feels uneasy and disoriented. To use the language of Goffman, there are few familiar props to hold on to; little or no evidence of an educational setting. Where the visit was a result of parents refusing to respond to letters from the school or, more generally, where the parent is unsure about what the teacher is doing in the home, there is more likelihood that parents will also feel uneasy and interpret the visit as a slight on their parenting skills.

Jim Craig, another cooptive teacher, was one of the few teachers to adopt home visits as an integral part of his teaching remit by setting aside one night a week to visit parents. He adopted a crusading approach to his job in his advocacy of stronger parent–teacher links.

> I'm setting up projects, contacting families that will be involved, work experience, social skills type things. I'm talking through the difficulties that exist at school and how I saw things developing within the school. If they [truanting pupils] continued attending, the kinds of alternatives that I could offer . . . see if I can get an agreement with them to stay at school or take up the offered alternative.

Sometimes even his skills as educational mediator were severely tested. On one occasion he had visited a parent whose son was causing problems in class. He commented on how he was received by the parents.

> [They were] initially a bit defensive. A recent one was a woman who was quite insistent that she wasn't going to listen to me until she'd had a cup of coffee. I was doing the job of the guy from the pools coming to offer them a million pounds. She wasn't interested in that. She thought I was going to give her a hard time. There was a lot of resistance. It took a while to realize that I was being quite nice and offering her something.

From the teachers' perspective the lack of familiarity with the individual parent or parenting couple's environment acts as an important check on the professionalism of the teacher. But the boundaries of their educational roles are tested in more familiar circumstances, when parent–teacher meetings take place in school. The invasion of parental territory is just as sensitively picked up by teachers when the subject of discipline is brought up. There is some variation in the degree of teaching self-consciousness which again relates to the kinds of approaches that are made by parents and teachers. Where parents actively solicit advice from teachers on how to discipline their children, the meeting can be sustained without a great deal of hostility and suspicion from the parent. There is also a sense in which the teacher is more at ease here as parents unburden their problems. Norah Bowles, who had earlier argued that teachers should not be put in the position of advising parents about how to discipline their children, only felt comfortable in this advisory role where the parent was openly asking for guidance. But even this was tempered by the fact that as a young teacher she couldn't really be expected to know how to solve a parent's problems.

> They'll often say, what do you think? There are quite a lot of money problems. How much should he give him? I'll say, 'He doesn't need two pounds a day. He'll get a good school meal for sixty pence.' More often they'll say, 'I cannae do a thing with him. I've tried everything. I don't know what I'm going to do next.' Most of the time I can't think of things for her to do.

These meetings are normally much easier for both parties where there is a lot of communication between the home and the school; where parents and teachers strike up 'working relationships'. This approach was adopted by two 'cooptive' teachers.

> I'll discuss discipline when it's on the agenda. It's a very delicate issue . . . need to establish a relationship before I'm prepared to point out these things. (Joan Leslie)

> I use the phone a lot. I have constant communication with parents that have asked me to keep an eye on their child. Parents often phone me. I have lots of communication with parents. (Anne Smart)

Given that the majority of teachers tended to identify behavioural and educational problems in familial terms, and given that within the school they are expected to act on the information they have on the child, the discussions with parents tended to reach critical points where the subject of parental sanctions becomes unavoidable. Where they know the parent and where they are asked for advice, the meeting can be dealt with relatively harmoniously. But most of the teachers are at their most uncomfortable when they are put in a position of having to offer unsolicited advice to parents on how to bring up their children. This potentially sets up a conflictual relationship between the parent and the teacher as both parents and teachers become more conscious that the boundary between the legitimate responsibilities of parents and teachers is being threatened. Teachers often skirted around the subject of parental discipline.

> I'd ask leading questions like 'Does he have a lot of friends?' 'Does she go out a lot at night?' and, do they know where she is going? and leave it to them to deduce that I don't quite approve of that. I wouldn't see it as my role to advise them. (Susan Bruce)

Another approach adopted by a few of the teachers was to confront the parent with the problem. Ian Howe would involve the child in the discussions as a way of convincing the parent that *this* child is *their* responsibility.

> *MW*:   Do you ever discuss their disciplinary role?
>
> *IH*:   Yes. I have the pupil present as well. Sometimes the parents want to talk about a problem in the home and they ask wee Johnny to leave. Maybe that's why there's a problem at home because the boy isn't involved in trying to find a solution. I often have to confront parents.
>
> *MW*:   How do they react?
>
> IH: It's mixed. Some go on the defensive. Some will acknowledge what I'm saying and quite often parents agree.

Ross Stewart used 'shock' tactics in trying to convince the parents of what he saw was the self evidently inadequate role of particular parents. The transcript is worth reproducing in full.

> *RS*:   Different members of staff have different methods. What I tend to do is I have a report. I tend to take out all the adverse comments made by all the teachers concerned and list them. I'll sit there and say 'unruly, disgusting, inattentive etc'. I'll read out a list of twenty or so of these adjectives and I'll say to the parents, do you know who this describes? These are comments made by colleagues about your 13-year-old son or daughter. I'm describing your daughter to you as a group of professional people. They'll say, 'Oh, I didnae ken it was that bad. He's no' like that at haim, he's a nice wee laddy.'[2]
>
> *MW*:   Is there ever any hostility?

RS: Occasionally I'll get hostility and sometimes I'll converse with my head teacher first before approaching them. But I've never had parents who have remained hostile all the way through the meeting. I don't think I've ever had a parent leave here in a hostile mood.

MW: Do you discuss parents' disciplinary roles?

RS: We ask them quite often directly, what sanctions do you use at home? Sometimes they use very few sanctions. We'll suggest that they stop the pocket money or suggest they are in by, say, half past eight. At the same time you discover a family breakdown by talking to the parents. You ask them, well what about meal time. 'Oh, we never eat together. When the father comes home he wants to sit down with his beans and chips and watch the television. He's no' interested. Wee Johnny, he'll no eat with us. He's always out playing.' So you have this breakdown where at no time do they ever deliberately draw the family together to form relationships.

He recounted another meeting.

We had one case [we can talk about this more freely because she left school a few years ago], a really well developed girl who was causing a lot of trouble within the school. We called the parents in. The parents' reaction was, 'She's an awfy nuisance at home and we give her money to go out'. I asked them, 'Do you never wonder about the rising statistics on attacks on young girls?' This girl at the age of 15 was all dolled up and could be mistaken for 17 or 18. The parents' answer to this indiscipline at home was to give her a fiver and send her out for the night because that gave them peace and quiet.

Overambitious Parents

Guidance, as most of the teachers continually pointed out, was often misconstrued as discipline in its negative guise. Although the National Curriculum has largely circumscribed any notion of curriculum choice, one of the 'positive' guidance responsibilities was to help pupils select the subjects they would take for the duration of their school careers. The subject choice process (SCP) is particularly relevant to this study in that the target age of the respondents' children was 14 or 15, the age at which they would be choosing their subjects. It was, therefore, of particular relevance for the parents as well as the teachers. The SCP is of interest because there are parallels with the process of defining classroom indiscipline in terms of problem parents. More directly, although the SCP doesn't follow a symmetrical pattern with the disciplinary process, in certain respects the teachers define certain parents, intimately involved with the school through the SCP, as problems. These are what I term 'overambitious' parents.

Let us consider the differences between the absent parent and the overambitious parent. Firstly, whereas the former is a result of a lack of communication with the school, the latter is a result of the opposite, communication which is over and above what the teachers see as legitimate parental involvement. The parents' meetings where the subjects are discussed are seen by the school as an important indication of the degree of parental support for their children's educational well-being. As with all meetings parents are actively encouraged to take part. Yet, the subject choice meetings, unlike the meetings that teachers have with 'absent' parents, are fundamentally about the educational well-being of the child. As well as having expertise in their own fields, guidance teachers act as mediators between the parent and the relevant subject teachers. Guidance teachers also give parents an overall picture of what the child would be best advised to do in relation to what that child is capable of, and what the child wants to do. In theory, the choices that are made are informed by the child's performance in school rather than any imputed behavioural pattern exhibited within the home. No matter how motivated teachers are in out-of-school terms, they have much less control of the interactional settings where teachers engage with absent parents. Where the meetings take place at designated times within school, and where the discussion centres around the educational well-being of the child, the teacher has the upper-hand.

A second and related difference between absent and overambitious parents is the absence of other social agencies. Moving up the disciplinary system with absent parents means formalizing the problem by linking up with the educational welfare officer, the social worker and sometimes the police. Although the problem child is brought to the attention of the teacher as a problem pupil, the further up the disciplinary hierarchy the child goes, the more likely the problem will be dealt with in non-educational terms: the more problematic the child becomes the less appropriate the teaching role becomes in solving the problem. Difficulties that arise through the SCP, on the other hand, are managed solely by the teachers.

Problems arose when parents questioned the educational criteria laid down by the school. Parents sometimes disagreed with the school's advice on what subjects their child should take. These difficulties tended to surface more in 'high achievement' schools. Teachers from Stenhouse Academy and Logan High – schools within more deprived areas and with falling school rolls – had fewer problems with parents who questioned the advice given to them by the school. The following teachers were asked about overambitious parents.

> We don't get many like that. Our choices are limited here . . . we don't have many parents as meticulous enough to come up to the school and insist that their child do this or go to another school. (George Barry, Logan High)

> Not really. They sometimes have unrealistic ideas about what their kid can do. My husband works in another school which is totally different and he has a lot of these kinds of parents. (Ruth Smith, Stenhouse Academy)

Although there is no hard evidence to back this up, the problem of overambitious parents appeared to be more prominent in the other three schools. When asked what criteria she used when discussing the subject choice with parents, Vivien Willis from Waterston replied:

> The wishes of the child . . . career interests of the child . . . their apparent strengths and weaknesses. I think that parents tend to be overambitious for their kid. We have had some very unhappy experiences where children have been put into classes to which they were patently not suited. They were taken there more or less screaming. There have been disasters.

Within these terms the best interests of the child can only really be assessed by the teachers.

Overambitious parents, then, are those who are perceived to be interfering with the educational process. This is not expressed directly by the teachers in terms of a rejection of their advice, but in how parents are going against what is best for their child in pursuit of their own ambitions as parents. Teachers picking up these signals have a difficult task in trying to persuade parents that it is the child that is the focus of attention.

> Some parents try to force their ambitions on their children. This happens quite a lot. It's really a case of trying to convince them that if you look at their grades and the comments . . . You have to try and persuade them that they're not suitable for certain subjects and would perform better in something they're good at or like. (Mary James)

To a certain extent the introduction of the standard grading system for some teachers meant that this was less of a problem. Standard grading widened the scope for educational attainment in that it allowed children to achieve at a lower level of attainment that previously had not existed.[3]

> All the time, parental expectation doesn't match up with the reality most of the time. Pushy parents wanting their kids to do certain things and their kids aren't up to it. It's changing a bit with the introduction of standard grades. The standard grade offers kids the choice of working at an appropriate level. It was a big problem in the past. Parents wanted their kids to do 'o' grades and it wasnae on. (Jim Craig)

In the end, the school does require the parent's signature on the subject choice form. For Bill Short, the assistant head at St Mary's, it is the parent who decides.

> The school has always adopted the policy that ultimately the parent should decide. We'll only recommend a course of action. We can say that there's no chance that this kid will get these subjects, but it's ultimately up to the parents. We're sometimes able to persuade them of the best course of action.

Teachers have various ways of coping with a situation where their professional advice is superseded by 'parental ambition'. The meetings can be stretched out over a period of weeks as teachers try and persuade parents that their children won't cope. But the advantage the teacher has over the parent – the knowledge the teacher has of the child's performance – is usually quite effective in bringing parents around.

One final point concerns the management of the boundary between the home and the school asserted by the teachers. Earlier in the chapter we discussed how teachers tended to think that mothers were responsible for linking up with the school in disciplinary matters. It may be worth differentiating between significant and routine aspects of 'boundary maintenance' here (La Fontaine, 1990). Mothers may dominate in routine matters, this was not the case with less routine matters such as the SCP. The teaching impression here was that fathers were more actively involved in discussions with the school over their adolescent child's academic future and were as likely as the mother to sign the subject choice form. Dorothy Smart summed up this view.

> If you want a general feeling, the father tends to be the one that pushes the child to do the academic course. The pressure is more from the father to the academic subjects, the mother tends to advise the child not to take on too much at the one time.

When asked who tended to be involved on the SCP, Ian Howe stated:

> Both. Fathers take a greater interest at this stage in their child's education than any other stage. Mothers will come to normal meetings but at S2 father will come as well.

Conclusion

There is no escaping the importance attached to parental primacy by both parents and teachers. In the construction of a model relationship between parent and teacher, stress was placed on the disciplinary role of the parent as the moral and social guardian of the child's development. Paradoxically, the division between discipline and education was sharpened by the lay social theories expressed by teachers about the origins of problem children in school.

An expanding guidance network gave teachers a much clearer picture of the kinds of problems that some parents faced in being able to control and discipline their children. Guidance teachers were immersed within an institutional framework which focused their attention on the family backgrounds of these children. Primacy here was affirmed through its marked absence. What they saw and experienced from time to time, through their roles as mediators between home and school, were parents who did not conform to any notions of inner direction or parental authority.

It was these types of parents that guidance teachers had to deal with in satisfying the more abstract notion of the pupil's best interests.

Possibilities of intervention may be legitimated through lay theories of social class. In some schools, where there may be a collective sense of local deprivation, teachers take a more surrogate role on the basis of the class complexion of the parents. But, in general, the assumptions that teachers made about the *familial* nature of the problem restricted the form that their actions took towards dealing with the problem child.

The highly sensitive nature of 'disciplinary talk' in school between parent and teacher was reflected: firstly, in the difficulties some teachers had in dealing with unsolicited requests for advice; secondly, in the ways that teachers tried to elicit information about discipline in the home without seeming to questions the parent's authority; and thirdly, by parents themselves who adamantly claimed that discipline within the home was not on the teacher's agenda at parents' meetings.

Where there was a tradition within the local community of close links between the school and the parent, teachers found it much easier to set up contacts with parents who were having difficulties with their children. In these situations, guidance teachers found it much easier to define their responsibilities as complementary social supports to parents rather than as surrogate parents.

The previous chapter suggested that teachers can be categorized according to two criteria; the kinds of schools that the teachers belonged to and the different techniques used in controlling classroom behaviour. The former was important in determining the ease with which teachers were able to handle these perceived forms of intervention. Where there were few ties with the local community and where the local community had a high level of social deprivation, teachers were more inclined to see themselves in more negative terms as picking up the pieces from parents who had apparently abdicated their responsibilities.

The reverse of this was found in the schools where parental expectation was high in terms of pupil achievement. Guidance teachers were playing what they considered to be a more legitimate role in providing an intellectual and emotional support to existential adolescent problems of development. They were also more active in providing the educational backup during the subject choice period which, in effect, provided the occasion for a demonstration of their educational skills. Yet, like the absent parent the overambitious parent served the purpose of affirming the division of responsibility between home and school in that these parents from time to time intervened within what was considered the teacher's locus of responsibility in claiming that they knew more about their children's educational capabilities than the school.

Notes

1 Although parents are legally entitled to educate their children at home, the conditions and circumstances surrounding this position are so exceptional that very few parents

would consider this a viable option. Certainly, no parent from the sample expressed this as an option.

2 dinnae ken = do not know; haim = home.

3 An important educational debate in Scotland in the early 1980s took place over the relevance of the examination system. It was argued that a significant number of 14- and 15-year-old pupils were excluded from gaining any form of tangible benefit from the school. Standard grading was a pre-national curriculum attempt to deal with this problem by introducing a foundation level of attainment. See Meikle's article, 1980.

Chapter 4

Parenting, Supervision and the Uncivil Society

Introduction

The previous chapters deal with the way in which discipline is handled within educational context. In this chapter I look at the ways in which parents discipline and control their children within the 'privacy' of the home. The first part of the chapter takes a more negative line in respect to disciplinary matters by looking at how parents sanction their children when they step out of line. Yet, as was discussed earlier, discipline does not have to be conceptualized solely in terms of repression. The concept of discipline tends to connote images of the intolerant, strap-wielding patriarch but a more positive image of the parent as disciplinarian is presented here. Discipline is seen as the means by which parents are able to set boundaries within which children develop a sense of moral and psychological security.

Discipline, then, is bound up with the general welfare of the child. In the second part of the chapter this is examined with reference to ideas parents have about how their adolescent children conduct themselves outside of the home. I argue that this in turn shapes the way that parents try to supervise their children's public activities. The previous chapters emphasized the normative and common-sense restrictions placed on the school in underwriting the child's moral and social welfare. Although the structure of the school encourages a more holistic attitude towards the child, the particular frame of reference adopted by both parents and teachers here has been the separation of the spheres.

The following analysis outlines the accounts parents give of their children's developing moral characters and identifies a shift in the parental frame of reference. The following two chapters revolve around the development of their children's sexual identities. In this chapter, notions of moral danger underpin the perceptions that parents have of their children's time spent away from the home. In both cases the school's moral and social role becomes more central. This inevitably points to a more complex relationship between parent and teacher than was suggested in the 'separate spheres' model discussed earlier.

Authority, Sanctions and Adolescence

The previous chapter demonstrated the widely held belief that parents ought to circumscribe their children's views of the world in one form or another. Although the Weberian notion of a rational authority opens up the theoretical possibility for a more open and negotiable relationship between parent and child, there is still a strong sense that parents are ultimately trying to maintain an obedient relationship between themselves and their children (Hood-Williams, 1990). Some parents expressed a degree of confidence about the authority they had over their adolescent children, whilst others tended to think that adapting to the child's adolescent status was a problem. In the former case, parents were able to discuss with confidence the kinds of sanctions they used when their adolescent children stepped out of line. Six parents claimed that their children knew how far they were able to go; raising their voices was usually enough to bring them back into line (five middle class: one working class). If we look at two middle-class examples of more verbal approaches to misbehaviour, we can see that although parents might step back from adopting the imperative 'thou shalt not' form, they were, nevertheless, very conscious of how their authority as disciplinarians had to be firmly asserted. Brian Slany claimed:

> They need to understand the reason for it [the sanction]. We've always brought them up to have a choice. If you want to do it your way you've got to be aware of the consequences. If you want to do it my way well fair enough. If they're misbehaving unless its a major thing, then there's no choice. Invariably they're told the privileges they've got will stop. That's been sufficient. I've always believed that discipline is needed from a very early age. They've always respected me for discipline. They do occasionally step over the line but they are always aware that they are stepping over the line, so they never go too far. A word from myself and they step back.

He went on to emphasize the choice his children had in accepting the rules which were instilled very early on.

> I encourage them to be their own selves, so, sometimes they do step over the line. Sometimes I'll have to talk to them about it, but I have no fears. They have their own personalities and I've developed that with them.

Brian Slany comes close here to the notion of inner direction in that there is explicit reference to how a child's individuality is secured by stressing the importance of discipline.

Bob Alison, placed more emphasis on the generational notions of respect and deference. Children could be made to understand why their parents had sanctioned them but this didn't necessarily lead to a lessening of the 'distance' between father and child.

> MW: What are the situations when you discipline Peter [oldest son]?
>
> BA: He's cheeky, the same as any other lad. He has a bad habit of not waiting 'till you've finished talking and launching in. Probably talking back although it's probably less that and more trying

to explain why he's done something wrong! Every kid does things that niggle their parents. As long as you try to bring them round to thinking that, that is not the way to do things, not enforcing them . . .

MW: Do you try and reason with them?

BA: Oh no, I don't reason with him. I mean if he's said something he shouldn't have said then he's told and then he's told why. It's not something we'd sit down and discuss. I don't believe in children telling their parents or other adults what they should be doing. I'm not into them saying you do this or talkin' in any way disrespectful.

Parents found it difficult to answer questions about the efficacy of the more material sanctions used. Some parents tended to see the preference they had for a particular sanction in terms of the degree to which it worked. Yet, rather than being seen as ways in which misbehaviour can be diminished, they were seen primarily as punishments. One of the main effects of sanctions was that they were meant to hurt. Although their eldest son, Philip, was proving to be a bit of a handful, the Wilsons were able to handle him by 'grounding' him, that is, depriving him of his free time outside of the house.

We have problems. He [Philip] hates to be kept in. He likes to get out all the time. Obviously if I say he has to stay in, that's that. That's what discipline is all about. (George Wilson)

This was reinforced by his wife.

You get to know your kids . . . the most punishing thing for Philip is to be kept in . . . he tends to push it a wee bit further and he knows he's to come in at 10.30 . . . He came in on Saturday night. It was 11.15 when he came in. Without discussing it George said 'You are in all day tomorrow.' That is punishing to Philip. (Jean Wilson)

Another sanction, the withdrawal of pocket money, was seen by Janice White and Isobel Hart's children as a deprivation. Janice White was asked about her children's reaction to losing their pocket money. She replied:

They weren't amused. They were hard up that week. They just didnae get it. They had tae do without.

A similar response came from Isobel Hart:

The best way to deprive him [her son] is tae stop his pocket money and pit him in his room.

Parents also emphasized the ineffective nature of certain sanctions in terms of how they didn't work as punishments. Although grounding was a popular sanction, parents that favoured other forms tended to argue that keeping a child at home was ineffective where a child preferred to stay at home rather than play outside with friends. When June Wilkins was asked whether she ever grounded her eldest son, she replied:

> He's no' a laddy for going out. I think I'd be penalizing him if I sent him out! He's a computer freak so I take that away sometimes.

Problem Children or Problem Phase: A Case Study

Given the existing pressures on parents, and the 'private' nature of their responsibilities, we might expect a degree of self-censorship or 'fronting' where parents are asked to account for discipline within the home (Goffman, 1969). The Terrys, for whatever reason, chose to discuss the problems they were having dealing with their oldest son's behaviour (the Wilsons, similarly, later in the chapter).

As I stated earlier, there is no necessary contradiction between the concepts of childhood and independence. Childhood can be seen as a preparation for the real world of social responsibility and commitment. Yet reconciling earlier parenting routines with an awareness of the changing nature of childhood for some parents is beset with problems. This is exemplified by the Terrys.

MW: What do you do for sanctions?

GT: We keep asking him, keep plugging away. We don't make an issue of it. We don't really forget it either.

MW: Do they listen to you?

GT: They get very upset if we're annoyed. But they tend not to do anything about it.

MW: What would you do then?

GT: Shout at them I suppose.

MW: Do you send them to their rooms?

GT: I do that as well

MW: Effective?

GT: Not really. It doesn't stop them doing it.

In the previous section, parents claimed that they had developed methods for dealing with their children's misbehaviour. From this perspective we might echo the sentiments of one teacher that parents have 'got the measure' of their children because they were able to gauge what were the most appropriate and 'painful' sanctions to be used when their children stepped out of line. George Terry might be said to have failed because he didn't know his children well enough.

Although this may, indeed, be the case, the issue is complicated when a parent feels that a child has reached the age where misbehaviour might be more explicitly related to adolescence. The lack of understanding that George Terry had of his children might be interpreted more positively as recognition of the changes in his children's development – the move towards asserting their own individual identities. Within these terms, George Terry was having difficulty adjusting his disciplinary approach accordingly. Although George Terry seemed resigned to having little impact on his children's behaviour, his wife hinted at the problem being one of adjustment to her oldest son's attempts at asserting himself as an individual with reference to her own value system.

> The eldest one, he has now taken to questioning your values as it were. We're sitting down to a meal in peace. He'll say, 'Why should you do this? Why shouldn't you get up in the middle of the meal and do something else?' It's a difficult one. If you've got values it's difficult to justify them – they're so deep rooted and taken for granted. Why shouldn't you take your meal into the front room – all his friends do it, sort of idea. This is quite a conflict at the moment. (Christine Terry)

The problem of controlling her children has become more acute because her oldest son is now perceived to be questioning the norms of behaviour that she takes for granted. Although this is not made explicit in the quotation, we might speculate on the nature of Christine Terry's problem. Once Christine Terry had detected the beginnings of an 'adult' personality in her eldest child, any misbehaviour becomes more difficult to deal with. When her children were much younger her role as a disciplinarian had a much clearer *raison d'être*. As is expressed by parents in the following section, young children need more direct and explicit guidance in learning the rules of behaviour. Sanctions have a legitimate role to play in setting a moral agenda within the home. The problem for Christine Terry is that this disciplinary role becomes more difficult to sustain when the child reaches adolescence. Children are assumed to have a reasonable idea of the moral boundaries, this in part being a central feature of their developing independent characters.

We can talk, as Rapoport, Rapoport and Strelitz (1977) do, of the necessity of guiding the adolescent child through tricky moral terrain. But the means by which parents achieve this are more difficult to identify. Moreover, the role of the parent as disciplinarian sits uneasily with parents who feel that their children are too old for more direct and explicit forms of discipline. In one sense, Christine Terry interprets her son's misbehaviour as a symptom of an underdeveloped sense of the moral boundaries – the outcome of years of unsuccessful striving by parents to instill a moral code. In another sense, Christine Terry's anxieties are caused by her son's ability to undermine her values *because* he is reaching a stage in his life where his own identity reflects a vague sense of values which are different from her own.

The Use of Force

Although current debates over physical punishment within the home have focused on whether smacking should be abolished *per se*, a common assumption made is that physical punishment becomes a progressively less important sanction as children get older.[1] The extent to which parents show an awareness of their child's adolescence might be better assessed, then, in terms of the extent to which parents still draw on force as a sanction. Although the majority of parents no longer regularly used force within the home, fourteen parents (32 per cent) claimed to occasionally raise their hands against their adolescent children when they got out of hand. If we allow for the greater numbers of middle-class parents, there is no significant difference along social class lines in the numbers who use force (nine middle class: five working class). Physical punishment tended to be administered as a spontaneous reaction to a particular incident that annoyed a parent. But one or two parents still used force as part of a repertoire of sanctions. When asked what she did when both her adolescent children were badly behaved, Betty Deary, a part-time home help, replied:

> Do you want me tae tell ye? That slipper, there, and then up the stairs and to their beds. They get a good wallop.

In Tom Mctear's case it followed a series of threats.

> Although I tend to shout a lot at them, I always threaten as well. I very seldom carry it through. I'm not against kids getting their backsides skelped when they need it. That's what's wrong with them nowadays. If they keep talking back to me there is going to be some instant justice right there and then.

Yet, this view needs to be tempered by the lack of specificity over the particular children who were still being smacked. Tom Mctear, a policeman, later on in the interview signalled a change in relationship with his eldest son.

> With the best will in the world there comes a time when you can no longer tell them what to do. You've got to move from telling them to advising them. I've had this already with my oldest. I cannae now brow beat and tell him what to do. I can only say I don't think it would be wise to do this or that.

The Mctears had three children. Alistair, the oldest, was 18 years old and had just left home to join the RAF. The other children, still at home and at school, were younger. Although Tom Mctear was not signalling a change in his relationship with his adolescent child – his 15-year-old daughter was one of the younger children – there was a sense in which both father and eldest son had just come through a difficult adolescent period. Tom Mctear now seemed to accept that rather than impose his will through using force, he was now advising his son on the best way of doing things. Mctear, then, acknowledged the changing status of his children yet still tended to think that adolescent misbehaviour could be dealt with using a degree of force.

The Wilsons both agreed that smacking was only appropriate for small children. Nevertheless, the problems their eldest was causing occasionally pushed them into situations where they raised their hands. It is worth reproducing Jean Wilson's lengthy account of how she attempted to deal with Philip's behaviour because it identifies force as a reaction rather than part of any family policy on discipline.

> I've not sort of said I'm going to smack his behind but I have because they do drive you . . . I've lashed out at Philip. I've punched him before and I can see the day coming when George [her husband] and Philip will have a go at each other. Because Philip just in his manner . . . George will say something and Philip will make some smart remark. George will jump up. The two of them are standing there. I often think that if Philip was to go to lift his hand I could see a . . . you know . . . as for saying, 'I'm going to give him a doing', that's never happened. There's been the spontaneous slap or punch. Sometimes they're so cheeky. The other morning I went into Philip's room . . . of course the way the boys do their hair now. They have to have mousse and gel. I'm running a hotel and I've got to be kind of tidy when they go down there in the morning. I wash my hair and I keep my mousse under the sink. I can't find it. I go all the way through the hotel in my dressing gown to Philip's room to get my mousse. I start shouting at him and he turns to me. Instead of saying 'Sorry mum', he says, 'Have you got a brain?' I sort of picked up the mousse and threw it at him. It's over in a second.

What is interesting here is that parents were not really disciplining their adolescent children by hitting them. There was no sense here in which force was used as a means of training their children for adulthood. Rita Barnes, like Jean Wilson, would react by 'clouting' her son when she felt he was getting on her nerves.[2]

> I clout him from time to time for being cheeky . . . It's not really cheek. He tries to see how far he can go. He's quite funny actually. But sometimes I can't be bothered with him being funny.

Interestingly, Rita Barnes's husband recounted an incident he had with their son where he used force. The relationship here was almost 'adult' in character in that both father and son apologised for their conduct.

> We were just back from holiday and we fell out one night. It wasn't a smack – it was a slap. It was something that really got to me. It has to be something that I would tend to see as very serious before that would happen. Probably the last time I smacked him before that was two years ago a particularly bad thing which I blew up at and I lashed out at. I probably shouldn't have. As it turned out I apologised in the morning as he apologised to me as well. (Will Barnes)

'Training' tended to take place much earlier and was associated with smacking. Parents argued that very small children were only able to discriminate between right and wrong through smacking. Thirty-five parents (85 per cent) mentioned that they smacked their children when they were much younger. Very few parents ruled out corporal punishment in principle, but a majority of parents now felt it was inappropriate to lift their hand as a means of disciplining their adolescent children. This view was best exemplified by Alice Davies, when asked whether she ever smacked her children.

> When they were small, yes. When they were at the stage when they just didn't understand. If you tried to explain I mean if somebody is hurting somebody else, pulling the cats tail. If they're at an age where they can't understand what the cat's going through and you can't explain that it's hurting the cat, and it's not a very good thing to do, you've got to do something.

Elisabeth Johnston, saw an 'associative' benefit in smacking a very young child.

> I've smacked them both on very particular occasions and that was when they went out . . . when they both ran out onto the road without looking and it was dangerous . . . and I did it instantly so that it should feel traumatic. I have also smacked him when he ran away from me at Tescos and I looked for him and was very upset. I rationalized the smacking in terms of it's like going out onto the road. You really could have got picked up and taken away and this was a life threatening situation and you must never do this again.

Most parents argued that smacking was an inappropriate sanction for their adolescent children. The majority of parents who still occasionally raised their hands to their adolescent children saw this as a spontaneous response to incidents which had annoyed them. Parents tended to explain these as isolated incidents where their children had taken them way beyond their tolerance thresholds. But there is a more interesting possible explanation. The use of force reflected the general ambivalence that parents felt about sanctioning their teenage children. On the one hand, parents reacted to their children because they thought they ought to know better at their age. Force was being used ironically to illustrate the outmoded nature of the sanction. On the other hand, parents felt that their children had not quite reached adult-hood. Force, acted as a timely reminder that parents still have the upper hand.

Supervision and the Uncivil Society

As was discussed in Chapter 1, the outside world is a testing ground for the way that parents and adolescent children relate to each other. As children get older they spend more time away from their parents. Time taken to build up relationships with peers and other adults can be seen as part of the routine breaking of early parent–child ties. In a positive sense, children are learning to take responsibility for their actions. For some parents this is taken to mean that children behave in a more grown-up fashion with others outside of the home. Parents commented on the way their children conducted themselves in restaurants and in front of other members of the family. John White commented on how his children were able to hold their own in adult company: 'They're both witty laddies, telling jokes and dancing with the women at parties.' For others, this notion of the responsible child is problematic because this is bound up with general concerns parents have about how their children negotiate the outside world on their own. It is to this problem that I turn to now.

In Chapter 1, I outlined the problems that parents might have coming to terms with their children's public persona. External influences can put parents under considerable pressure because of the ways that a child's behaviour outside of the home is assessed in terms of the quality of parenting. Chapter 3 might be taken as some form of confirmation of this, in that teachers tended to see problem pupils in terms of their family backgrounds. As I have argued, theories about parental control would tend to focus on how these kinds of pressures might dictate the ways that parents disciplined their children. The work of Harris (1983) and Seabrook (1982) suggests that the kinds of pressures that parents were under would lead them to want to have more physical control over their children's whereabouts.[3] Translated into sanctions this would mean that parents tended to prefer to ground their children, keep them within their purview. This is taken up at the end of the chapter.

I want to now consider discipline and control in more general terms as the means by which those in authority are able to set a moral and social agenda. Undoubtedly, the way that parents and teachers deal with misbehaviour can be seen as an important means of instilling a moral code. But if we look more directly at the way that authority figures are able to dictate how children negotiate the social world, then we need to look at discipline and control as a more positive means by which authority is expressed. This section focuses on how discipline can be linked to the kinds of perceptions that parents have of their children's public behaviour and the way that these perceptions structure what we might term strategies of positive control (Wyness, 1994a).

Parents were asked whether they had any concerns about their children's behaviour outside of the home. Given that the book focuses on the alleged countervailing moral and social powers of the school, parents were asked first of all whether

Table 4.1: *Parental Worry about the School, by Social Class*

	Middle class	Working class	Total
Yes	13 (54)	9 (45)	22 (50)
No	11 (46)	11 (55)	22 (50)
Total	24	20	44

* Figures in brackets refer to percentages of parents within each social class category.

Table 4.2: *Parental Worry about the Outside World, by Social Class*

	Middle class	Working class	Total
Yes	14 (58)	9 (45)	23 (52)
No	10 (42)	11 (55)	21 (48)
Total	24	20	44

* Figures in brackets refer to percentages of parents within each social class category.

they worried about their children's behaviour at school. This was followed by a more general question about the outside world. The latter was designed to cover the public terrain outside of the home and the school. As Tables 4.1 to 4.4 show, around half of the parents worried about what their children did outside of the domestic purview. This is divided up into two areas; concern expressed about behaviour in school and behaviour with friends outside. It is also clear from Table 4.2 that these concerns were expressed by both middle- and working-class parents. Both groups of parents expressed the same reasons for their concerns in relation to the question on the outside world – parents were concerned here about the physical and moral security of their children.

Tables 4.3 and 4.4 suggest that mothers tended to worry more about their children's public behaviour than fathers. Mothers tended to spend more time with their children than their husbands did because they were around the home more than their husbands. Almost all fathers were in full-time employment compared to only 23 per cent of their spouses.[4]

The anxieties that both parents expressed over their children's well-being outside of the home is the focus of this chapter. Harris (1983) only assumed that mothers were more likely to worry than fathers. His thesis was based on the Newsons' work which, although claiming to be about parents, was in fact based on evidence from mothers only (Newsons, 1963; 1968; 1976). There is little evidence of paternal anxiety because fathers were not interviewed.

Furthermore, the overemphasis on the Newsons' study of early childhood obscures any understanding of possible changes in domestic arrangements as the children get older. This might make it likely that fathers became more anxious about their children's well-being because they have become more aware of their children's well-being. Although mothers were home more than fathers, their adolescent children spent more time outside of the home than they did when they were younger. Some corroboration of this comes from the responses that parents gave to the question: Do you see less of your children as they get older? Twenty-six parents

Table 4.3: *Parental Worry about the School, by Sex of Parent*

	Mother	Father	Total
Yes	12 (55)	10 (45)	22 (50)
No	10 (45)	12 (55)	22 (50)
Total	22	22	44

* Figures in brackets refer to percentages of parents within each social class category.

Table 4.4: *Parental Worry about the Outside World, by Sex of Parent*

	Mother	Father	Total
Yes	14 (63)	9 (41)	23 (52)
No	8 (37)	13 (59)	21 (48)
Total	22	22	44

* Figures in brackets refer to percentages of parents within each social class category.

(59 per cent) claimed that they saw less of their children now. The gender division is important with seventeen mothers and nine fathers saying yes. Mothers were around the house more when the children were younger. They were thus more likely to notice that their children were spending less time at home as they got older. Fathers who had less input when the children were younger did not necessarily notice the same difference. From this we might say that the decrease in time spent by mothers with their children brings them more into line with the amount of time spent by fathers with children. For many couples the times when their adolescent children were at home would tend to coincide more with the times that the father was home. Both parents were around for a greater proportion of the time that their children spent out of school. As I stated earlier, Harris based his argument on evidence drawn from work done with mothers and young children. If questions around parental anxiety were put to this category of parents we might expect there to be a greater disparity between mothers' and fathers' responses. As it is, the research focuses on parents of adolescents. Although more mothers than fathers worried about their children's behaviour outside of the home, more than a third of the fathers shared these anxieties. The following data then portrays the concerns that both mothers and fathers have.

In relation to concern over the school, there was some class difference. Middle-class parents tended to express concern about how their children's behaviour and the behaviour of others might inhibit their children's chances of educational success. Whereas, for working-class parents the concern was that their children were behaving properly. This can be demonstrated if we compare two responses from parents to the question: Do you ever worry about how your children behave in school? Rita Barnes, a care assistant in a nursing home, links her son's behaviour in class to his results.

> Oh yes, I do worry about it, but I've never had the occasion to think he is misbehaving. I would have heard from the school. His French teacher

says there's a lot of nonsense in the class. I've asked if William is one of them and she says he can be sometimes. But because of the results he's been getting, I'd tend to think that he is concentrating and behaving in the class.

For George Deary, a sheet metal worker, the behaviour of his children was what was important rather than any educational ends that it might facilitate.

Oh aye. We try tae thrash that home to them aw' the time, that they've tae behave well. Their total behaviour in everything. I mean we cannae make them saints but . . . on saying that I'm probably only one in about hundred parents. The wife and I are only one in a hundred families that'll do that.

Parental concern was more or less equally felt with respect to both the school and the outside world. Yet, unlike the outside world, the school was perceived differently in that parents had the potential to know indirectly through the teachers about the behaviour of their children. Rather than see this, as Harris (1983) does, as grounds for potential conflict between parents and teachers, several parents here were able to assuage their doubts about their children's behaviour by checking with teachers at parents' meetings. Evelyn Dobbie, a middle-class mother, expressed her worries.

I think about it. I often wonder. I can often imagine him at school, fooling about. That worries me sometimes because he could be distracting other people, he never stops talking. We've asked about it when we've been down at the parents' evenings but no great hassle, no' any great problem as he's getting older he's calming down and settling down. We've tried to get over to him how important this year is to him and get him to knuckle down. He doesn't seem to have any problems. We have asked at the school.

Again there is an emphasis on linking behaviour to educational performance. But here, also, some anxiety was expressed about referring to the teachers. The situation does potentially lead to the scenario put forward by Harris that children have the power to betray their parents through letting them down in front of the teacher. But the school is interpreted here by Evelyn Dobbie in much less conflictual terms. The school is used more as a resource to be draw on.

George Wilson, on the other hand, linked his children's public behaviour to their parenting role. He was asked why he worried about his children's behaviour at school. He replied, 'Because the school would think it was lack of discipline in the home.' George Wilson had given up a well-paid job with the bank to go into business with his wife. They had moved to another part of the city a year previously and were now running a small hotel. Initially, they had not moved Philip to a school within the new catchment area because they didn't want to disrupt his schooling and they were aware of the difficulties teenagers sometimes had breaking old ties and making new friends. Philip was eventually moved when he got into trouble with some other pupils.

> He was in a fight . . . we got a phone call from the school saying Philip was in trouble at the school. Philip and some wee laddy had fought in a park near the school. They were going to be suspended and we had to go to the school the next day. Both laddies apologised and said it wouldn't happen again. So we decided after that we'd get Philip transferred to Boreston. (George Wilson)

The move to Boreston enabled the Wilsons to 'keep tabs' on Philip because Boreston was much closer and he was able to come home at lunchtime. Moving school didn't solve all their problems, however. As his mother put it:

> Philip was being late quite a lot, even at Boreston – he was dawdling. They have a good system there. They phone you up in case he's not coming back and report it to you. We got really angry that the school should have to phone us up. He hadn't been telling us that he'd been continually late. We werenae aware of it because we had been sending him out in plenty time.

This point was reiterated by her husband. Their contacts with the school had increased at an unwelcome but, as George Wilson goes on to state, necessary speed.

> The teachers know that we're on their side. I've said that to the guidance teacher. We've said to her anything they do, no matter how small it is, phone us. We'd rather have stupid phone calls than nothing at all. We want to know what's going on.

The Wilsons were relieved that the school was able to keep tabs on Philip, but given the trouble he was causing the school, there was still a worry that people might think they had caused the problem. The Wilsons were very conscious of how others evaluated their roles as parents. But their anxieties motivated them to draw closer to the school in an effort to solve the problem of their son's misbehaviour. Clearly, some parents did express a concern about what the school thought of them as competent parents. This did to some degree offer evidence for Harris's thesis that parents worried about how the world outside perceived them. But as Wilson and Herbert (1978) argue in their study of parent–child relations in a deprived area, parents were also worried about what the outside world *did* to their children.

Allatt and Yeandle (1992) discuss the ways that parents redefined the moral order once their older children became unemployed. The moral order is associated with the outside world, a relatively ordered and secure space where children are morally bound by their work commitments. Allatt and Yeandle looked at how the trust the parents in their study placed in their children was threatened by unemployment. Children without the routine of work and the sense of commitment that goes along with work were more likely to drift into other more morally dubious public activities. Yet, this loss of trust was not based solely on notions of their children being unable to direct themselves towards more civic activities in the absence of employment. For what is being argued here is that the child finds it easier to develop this capacity for responsibility within a moral framework of guaranteed employment. Once this is taken away, parents question their children's abilities to negotiate the outside world because the outside world has become a more forbidding and alien environment. Allatt and Yeandle depict some conception of a moral environment through the images that parents convey of both the failure of their children to mature into responsible citizens and the lack of public means by which this might be achieved.

What is interesting here is that the children in Allatt and Yeandles' study had already experienced the possibility of a moral order through their early work experiences. The parents with adolescent children in this study were not able to draw on the experiences their children had of work. Parental anxiety in the present study was marked when discussing the world outside of the home and the school. This was a general area marked out by the streets and parks; areas which some parents asserted were *their* territories when they were young. The frame of reference, then, for these parents was not the world of work but the parents' own childhoods which were depicted as periods of relative safety where they had free rein over areas which were now blocked off from adolescent expression and play. As George Wilson stated, 'I'd love to see all the kids roaming the streets until midnight, but you can't.' These areas were problematic now because they didn't have the moral and physical security associated with their own past adolescent experiences.

It is worth mentioning here that the parents in this study probably had a much stronger sense of their responsibility towards their adolescent children than the sample in Allatt and Yeandle's study. The status of 'unemployed child' shifts the burden of responsibility away from the parent towards the moral order. As Jamieson and Corr (1990) point out, where children have some experience of work there was a much stronger sense of a contractual relationship between parent and child. Where children are contributing towards the household budget by paying digs, children probably feel that they have a much stronger right to do what they want with their free time. Parents, then, are in a much weaker bargaining position in trying to get their children to account for their movements outside of the home. Compared to the children in the Allatt and Yeandle study, parents in this study had a much stronger sense of their children *as* children.

Parents were in no doubt now about the dangers that lurked for their children on the streets. Almost all parents referred to these dangers. An interesting point was made by some parents who gave an assessment of their children's characters when discussing their children's peers and their external activities. Like some of the parents in Allatt and Yeandles' study, there was an implicit notion that some children are quite 'easily led'. The Harts, a working-class couple, were conscious of their son,

Thomas, getting involved with the wrong company. His father was asked whether he ever disapproved of Thomas' friends.

> I'll tell him that's him finished running around with him. It's no' very often like, but we've seen trouble with some kids and we've stopped him before he's followed suit. (Tom Hart)

His wife also worried about Thomas' choice of friends. She cited an example:

> There was an instance this morning. I got a phone call asking for Edward. I mean who knows that his middle name is Edward? It wis a wee lassie. Anyway I said Thomas was at school and I asked who was calling. She said, 'Veronica'. I said I'll give you two seconds to get off this line. The phone went again, 'Is David there?' So I just slammed the phone back doon. Thomas says, 'I cannae think, Mum, who that could have been.' If I thought he was getting up to anything like that, that wid really annoy me. If he was in a crowd using swear words or anything like that, I'd get really angry.

There is an issue here of whether the child can be trusted. Quite often parents' anxieties centred on their feelings that their children were immature, they were naive, not yet worldly enough to make the 'right' choices. Rita Barnes 'worried all the time' about her son. 'His chums are like him, too trusting.' This point was reiterated by Jim Short who claimed that his eldest daughter had to learn when to accept people at face value.

> I've chastised her a couple of times. I've told her you've got to be a wee bit two faced and know when to turn it on. I go on about how you should be in public crossing your 't's and how it can be different from how you are in private.

Jim Short believed his daughter had to learn how to manipulate the external world. There is almost a Goffmanesque critique of children here in having a naivety so out of place in a context where guile, diplomacy and a lack of trust are the moral hallmarks of the outside world. Yet, the self here is limited by the concerns of parents; for children apparently only need to 'turn it on' outside of the home. This interpretation of the self is a much more permissive version than Goffman's, yet is more constrained by the demands of parents. What we have here then is tangible concern being expressed by parents in moral terms over the physical well-being of their children.

Normal Misbehaviour

The parents' concern over their children's lack of cynicism in their relations with outsiders can also be identified through ideas parents have about common-sensical models of what constitutes good behaviour. Some parents emphasized the importance of being a 'good citizen'. Witness the following response by a parent to a question on aspirations.

> My main aim for him is that he becomes a decent citizen, someone I can be proud of, that he has respect for people and property. (Will Barnes)

Other parents invoked limits to the notion that their children needed to behave according to some bourgeois notion of gentile civility. Parents undermined the notion of civility by invoking 'normal misbehaviour'. In the conventional sense parents, teachers and public figures concern themselves over bad behaviour. Now it is true that parents did articulate ideas about how children ought to behave with reference to more conventional notions of respect or deference. But in conversation with some parents over their children's behaviour, and here we are specifically referring to boys' behaviour, parents have a concern that certain children were too good to be true. Parents had some intuitive notion of children who didn't quite fit in to a natural mode. There was an unspecified unease about certain children which couldn't be articulated in the more conventional language of the 'indisciplined child'. This unease was clearly articulated by Isabel Hart when discussing a friend of her son that she disapproved of.

> There was a wee boy who came to the house and he was that quiet. I thought there's nae wee boy that can be as quiet as that. I said to Thomas, 'I'm no' very keen on him son.' He said, 'How?' I said, 'He just seems awfy quiet.' He seemed too sweet to be wholesome. Now Thomas has been informing me after I'd told him not to go with him that he's into drugs. I said there was just something about the wee laddie, he wasnae a typical boy if you know what I mean, very withdrawn.

What is interesting is the initial assessment made of the boy being almost too well behaved. For Isabel Hart her fears were borne out by her son's friend's shadowy involvement with drugs (an interesting association between the withdrawn addict and the withdrawn child).

Parental Anxiety and Gender Identity

The existing literature on socialization (Sharpe, 1976; Newsons, 1976), suggests that boys are streamed into the public sphere of work through being relatively unsupervised outside of the home from an early age. Girls, on the other hand, learn about their future domestic responsibilities through identification with their mothers and this is reinforced by a gendered ideology. We would expect, then, that by the time children had reached adolescence, they would have a strong sense of their gendered identities, such that girls had little desire to roam the streets and boys would be constantly asserting their territorial rights outside of the home. There are two problems with this approach. First, both boys and girls spend a high proportion of their waking hours outside of the home. Research has suggested that the school streams boys and girls into different social spheres with fateful consequences for girls (Stanworth, 1981; Lees, 1993). But the simple fact that girls are on a par with boys in terms of the quantity of time they spend outside of the home in schools suggests that the gendering process is not quite as linear in the way that girls' domestic solitude prepares them for domestic labour. Second, if boys are encouraged to explore the social world outside the home as preparation for their public roles, rather than needing less supervision than girls they would appear to need more supervision. If girls have little desire to roam the streets – that is, they have been successfully 'socialized' into the domestic role – then the problem for parents might be how teenage boys are successfully able to negotiate the public world.

The following section on techniques of control can be read as confirmation of this in that parents tended to discuss how they would supervise their sons' external activities. Any quantitative assessment of this point is impossible because of the limited number of cases. But a few parents did worry that their daughters were getting into bad company. In the previous section I referred to Jim Short's daughter. I refer now to the case of Kathleen Bone, who at 14 years wanted to spend more time outside the home with her friends. This posed a problem for her parents who felt that she had started mixing with the wrong company. Her mother, Mary Bone, expressed her concern.

> We had a problem, that's why she changed school . . . with the friends she made. She was there at William Street school for three years. She had come from a small class of girls at primary . . . The way they split them up into classes – Kathleen was on her own. It was a shame, she was the youngest. They [the teachers] didn't think too hard about putting her in. They just threw her in with other kids she didn't know. She had to make her own friends and she's quite a shy girl. Obviously, she got over that. She got on in first and second year. She got friendly with children from Castleton [working-class area on the outskirts]. They wanted to go about just wandering the streets and we wouldn't let her. She was always taken to wherever she wanted to go and then taken back. They then asked her to go and play with them in the flats. We put our foot down and said no. From there it became worse. At first the teachers didn't notice it. These girls were really being nasty to her at the school. It got to the point where other teachers noticed it. I was up at the school three or four times . . . She was very unhappy, sometimes hysterical, and there were some nasty phone calls. So I said right, I'm taking her away from the school.

Several points can be made here. First, there was the same emphasis on the joint role played by parents and teachers in safeguarding the child's moral and physical well-being. Second, there was a strong emphasis placed on the parental purview; the children being chaperoned to and from their friends' houses. The concern being expressed here was the unsuitability of the streets and the dilapidated blocks of flats that the other girls played in. This point was reinforced by the father.

> In my opinion they're at an age where there is nowhere for them to go. They're too young to be hanging around street corners. Where does a 14 year old go?

Thirdly, both parents emphasized the distance between the home and their daughter's new school. As the school was not within the Bones' catchment area, there was an added difficulty of ensuring she got home from school safely. Finally, implicit in Mary Bone's statement was the notion that Kathleen was at some disadvantage vis-à-vis the rest of the girls. Kathleen was the youngest, she had been separated from her primary school friends and forced to make new friends. Kathleen was also, in her mother's words, not yet capable of looking after herself outside the home.

> We wouldn't let her play in those lifts. We said no, and she didn't want to. She thought that was wrong as well . . . She's a shy girl and wasn't able to fight back. She didn't like to be nasty to anyone. We were all upset about it.

Kathleen was in some sense, then, like the boys in the previous quotations, more easily led.

Schooling and Supervision

In the previous section both the Wilsons and the Bones exemplified the importance of links between the home and the school as a way of maintaining the physical and moral integrity of the child. Whether the problem originated within school or with peers outside, the emphasis is on parents and teachers working together.

A few parents were more specific in the range of responsibilities that they believed the school had in supervising their children. First, within a given time and space children were left in the care of the school whilst parents went about their daily routines. A corollary of this was that parents expected their children home from school at pre-designated times. Parents were very conscious of when the school closed and how long they expected their children to take to get home from school. Parents were quick to complain to the school if their children were being kept behind without their knowledge. One example of this is the concern parents expressed over the school's use of detention as a sanction. Children, particularly at St Mary's with a wide catchment area, relied on the school bus getting to and from home and school. Detention caused logistical problems because children had to stay behind after school and as a consequence had to make their own way home.[5] Bill Wilkins reflected many of the concerns over the uncivil society when discussing detention.

> I dinnae agree with detention because of our situation. If he's late from school . . . he goes to his granny's and his granny would worry . . . You're really feared for your kids at night, especially in the dark. There's a lot of

crazies gaun' about. Likes of when I was a kid we used to play to ten and eleven at night and our parents never worried because there was nothing to worry about.

Secondly, the school was seen to be indirectly responsible for policing the streets. In discussing the sanctions that were available to teachers, Jean Wilson felt that the school had a responsibility to keep troublesome children within school.

> I'd like to say right away that I don't approve of this suspension. Not that mine have ever been suspended, but they often talk about it. The teachers often threaten them with suspension. I've told mine if you were suspended I would take you along there every morning at nine. I would say to the head, here's my child for his education. They might tell me to take him away again, but I would be along there again the next morning. I don't agree with that at all. What are you teaching a kid by suspending him? They think, great. Some of the worst wee hooligans down in the west end were roaming the streets. They'd been suspended, maybe for fighting or something like that. They got a week's suspension. That's all wrong. You're better to have them where you can see them and see what they're up to.

This issue was picked up by some of the teachers. Teachers in general tended to argue that the most serious sanctions, exclusions and suspensions from school, were last resorts where the pupil had exhausted all other attempts by the staff to try and accommodate the pupils' problems within school.[6] Teachers tended to try and balance the interests of the school – the disruption that problem pupils caused in class – with the need to take firm action against the individual pupil where the school's rules had been breached. But these 'professional' concerns sometimes overlapped with a concern for public order. Teachers also worried about the consequences of exclusion for the pupil concerned and the local community. Ian Howe from Waterston High was asked about exclusions.

> IH: It's inevitable from the classroom situation. I think it's wrong to put pupils out of school unless alternative arrangements have been made.

> MW: But the region has a statutory obligation.

> IH: Yes, but that's not automatic. There's going to be a period of time when they are at no school and it's up to the parents to apply to the director of education to be reschooled. In my experience I've known pupils who've been excluded and I know of one who as early as S2 [second year of secondary school] was excluded and never went back to school. He started working with his father. He's well into his twenties now. He's a labourer-come-builder. He's never missed a day's work and he's never been out of work since being excluded. But in general I do worry about exclusions.

A third point made by parents stressed the playground as an area of potential danger. Bullying in school was a problem that parents were very aware of. Eight of the parents who worried about how their children behaved at school were concerned primarily about bullying (four working class: four middle class). Betty Deary, a working-class mother, was one in particular.

> I've had a wee bit of bother. I hav'nae been to the school about it, with Jean. She's been getting bullied quite a bit. The last day was only a fort-night ago and one or two of the girls had pushed her down the stairs and stood on her fingers. I said to her 'I'm going into the rector on Monday' . . . She's an easy going girl, she's very helpful, but she doesnae like gettin' picked on. They're there tae learn, no' tae be bullied aboot.

The concern over playground supervision was looked at from another angle by the Terrys. The problem here was the moral danger their children might find themselves in if left unsupervised by the school at lunchtimes.

> They (the children) can leave at lunchtime. When I was at school you weren't allowed out at lunchtime. It's not so much the danger. It's more the dinner money. They're (the pupils) given money . . . walking around the town being more interesting than school. There is some sort of lack here bearing in mind that you've got to send your child to school and they're (the teachers) in the positions of being parents while the child is at school. It's a hangup at the moment where teachers don't think certain things are their domain. Whereas if you're going to have a child in the school, you're responsible for that child until they come home. Not just for the periods when you think you are responsible for them.

'Keeping Tabs'

Buchner (1990), in a recent article, reflected the theme of parental decline, discussed in the first chapter of this book, when he argued that children are freer now from parental control because they spend more time outside of the home. Consequently, childhood had been 'individualized'; children's lives were less determined by adult influences. Two comments can be made. First, I have documented how parents in this study were conscious of the time that their children spent outside of the home. It didn't follow from this that adult control over children had disappeared. The concerns about their children's abilities to negotiate a dangerous outside world draws parents into a much more well-defined framework which emphasizes their children being in a given place at a given time. The school's supervisory respons-ibilities can be held up to more rigorous scrutiny. Concerns about the school on occasion become so acute that parents start to see the school as having primarily a 'baby sitting' function in keeping their children safe (Aviram, 1992). Given the input the school might have in the negotiation of the child's independence, we cannot say that children are left alone to negotiate their independence. Furthermore, we cannot assume that more time spent with peers meant that parents had less control over their leisure time.

Parents had no institutional means on which to fall back, where their children inhabited terrain outside of the home and the school. Yet, the overall sense of being in control of the child's moral and physical security is seen ultimately as a parental responsibility. This heightened sense of needing to know what the child is doing and where the child is doing it has lead to both middle-class and working-class parents adopting strategies for containing their children within their purview.

Parents suggested several ways of monitoring or 'keeping tabs' on their children. Several parents mentioned that they knew who their children's friends were; one or two knew the parents of these children. Ian Robbie was actively involved with what his sons did in their spare time.

> I know who Alexander goes about with. It's all to do with the rugby. I assist in coaching at the rugby club.

The Dobbie's concern was assuaged by knowing the kinds of friends that their son had because they had similar interests and dispositions.

> I often wonder what he's like. Is he any different from what he's like in the house? But there again his pals have got the same interests. Compared to some of them round here he's very quiet. He likes his pipe band, model railway and he's quite happy with his bike. He never goes about in a gang. (Evelyn Dobbie)

John Dobbie stressed a second way of keeping tabs on his son's activities; by keeping his son occupied. He was asked whether he worried over what his son did outside the house.

> I think about it but he's not a lad for the crowds. He tends to go with one or two pals. He doesnae hang about with a gang. He wouldnae be allowed – I'd put my foot down. We keep Michael's time pretty well occupied – he doesn't know it but if he had too much free time he would then go out looking.

According to John White, his eldest son was at the dangerous age of being receptive to the wrong type of external influences. Like the previous respondents, he was quite happy that his son was kept occupied by the Boys' Brigade which, although it took him away from home, was seen as an acceptable outside past-time. There was also a sense in which this was acceptable because his son's classmates were members.

> We'll tell them there are a certain couple of laddies I don't fancy. There's one in particular and I told him, 'Keep away fae him because', I says, 'aw' you'll get fae that laddie is trouble at school, trouble from the police.' The

laddie has been in trouble with the police after we'd told Jim to stay away . . . the younger one is no' at that stage yet . . . Jim is at the age now where it's awfy easy to get caught it in a thing like that. If you run with the pack you've got to do what the pack says. Ye' know what I mean. He's lucky he's got the BBs [the Boys' Brigade]. The more sensible type of laddie goes to the BBs. A lot of his mates go from Boreston.

The Boys' Brigade was not only see as a means of keeping him off the streets, it was a way of integrating the child into the moral order (Allatt and Yeandle, 1992).

Parents would also refer to a vast array of what Greenfield (1984) called 'electronic babysitters' (1987, p. 144). Several parents mentioned their children having televisions, stereos and computers in their rooms. Children's leisure time seemed to be much more easily accommodated within the home.

Nevertheless, parents were conscious of ties that their children made outside of the home and that it became much more difficult to keep them occupied as they got older. This was not a problem for a minority of parents whose children had little desire to go out and play on the streets. But where children liked the company of their friends outside of the home, parents quite often encouraged their children to bring their friends into the house (Newsons, 1976, p. 219). This is not simply a combination of knowing their friends and keeping them occupied; parents often didn't know all of their children's friends. Almost all of the parents at one time or another had disapproved of a particular friend. But as Jean Wilson stated, they were very seldom turned them away.

We try to encourage them to bring their friends into the house so that we can approve or disapprove of them. They are more or less allowed to bring anyone in.

This seemed an acceptable price to pay for keeping tabs on their children and discouraging them from engaging in activities they had little knowledge of. Parents were more likely to tolerate children they might not wholeheartedly approve of if their activities were confined within the home. The street if you like, was brought into the home where parents were able to keep an eye on who their children were associating with.

Sanctions and Supervision

I argued earlier that parents tended to link their favoured sanction with the ability to punish their children. But there is also an interesting connection between the forms of sanctions that parents adopt and the desire to keep an eye on their children. As we can see from Table 4.5, grounding was the most popular sanction with nineteen parents (43 per cent) claiming they preferred this to other forms of sanctions. Allowing for the greater number of middle-class parents, it was also a more common sanction among middle-class parents.

Table 4.5:   Type of Material Sanctions Used by Parents, by Social Class (N = 32)

Sanction	Middle class	Working class	Total
Grounded	13	6	19
Restricted to bedroom	2	4	6
Withdrawal of TV/computer	2	4	6
Withdrawal of pocket money	1	4	5
Withdrawal of food	–	1	1

* This list doesn't include sanctions such as force, threats and other more personal forms such as the raising of the voice.
** The table sets out the number of parents who mentioned a particular sanction. The overall total of responses does not match the total number of parents because eleven parents mentioned more than one sanction.

Pocket money, on the other hand, was not something that figured heavily in parents' calculations as to how they would sanction their children. Seventeen couples regularly gave their children either pocket money or an allowance. Yet, only five parents stopped their children's pocket money as a sanction. At the beginning of the chapter I pointed to the utility of stopping pocket money as a sanction. Parents were also concerned to express reasons why they didn't stop their children's pocket money. Parents argued that by depriving children of their pocket money they would be depriving themselves of a central axis of parental supervision. Parental supervision was linked to sanctions in three ways. First, parents tended to use the money they gave their children as a way of supervising what their children did with their pocket money. John Dobbie's son worked for him in his garage and was paid an allowance. He was asked whether his son could spend his allowance on what he wanted. He replied:

> He does control it. We keep an eye on what he's doing. If we think he's doing it wrong we try and explain it to him. It's very difficult to explain savings to a youngster, but he's doing all right. If he blew it that was it. There was no more after it. At the end of the week if he spends all his money he doesnae get school dinners.

Parents may be less likely to stop their children's pocket money where it was linked to the development of their children's budgeting skills. A second possible explanation rested on more general concerns that a few parents had about the possibilities of their children seeking unregulated leisure outside of the home if deprived of their pocket money. Christine Terry, who had earlier complained about lunchtime supervision in schools, was asked about what she did when her three sons misbehaved.

> Stopping pocket money . . . it would upset him. But I'm worried that if you cut off their pocket money they might try and acquire it some other way. I feel it's a rather debatable method to use.

There is here, then, an unease about what her children would get up to if they were deprived of their pocket money. Unlike the situation where the Dobbies were able

to closely monitor what their children did with their money, the Terrys were concerned that this lack of supervision would not only hinder attempts at making their
children more economically responsible, it would reduce their ability to supervise
their children's behaviour outside of the home.

Finally, a preference for grounding children may reflect the concerns that some
parents had about their children's moral and physical security outside of the home.
Where parents were concerned with how their children behaved outside the home,
any misbehaviour may be dealt with more comfortably by parents by confining
their children within the home. Thus, whereas from a parental perspective there is
a strange logic at work in the school expelling troublesome pupils, parents might
be more likely to place more of an emphasis on spatial restrictions for indisciplined
children.

Conclusion

In this chapter I have highlighted the difficulties parents faced balancing the
demands of responsibility for their children's well-being and any awareness of adolescent self-development. In discussions with parents over sanctioning approaches,
authority takes precedence over any concerns over the adolescent's autonomy. The
way that parents organize a code of behaviour within the home appears to rest on
the means by which parents are able maintain a hold over what their children are
allowed to do. So much so, that, in some cases, any talk of parents and children
negotiating household rules is seen as a dilution of their authority.

Where there was any concession shown to the adolescent's desire for autonomy,
this was in relation to the use of force as a sanction. A majority of parents saw force
as an inappropriate disciplinary mechanism to be used against their adolescent children. Nevertheless, although physical punishment was seen to have little moral or
educative value, where it was used it served to reaffirm the 'positional' difference
between parent and child.

We might ask ourselves at this point whether a parental desire for control
reflects an inability to come to terms with the child's move away from the immediate locus of parental authority. We might also ask whether the assertion of parental
control reflects a problem that parents have coming to terms with the myriad of
external influences that converge on parents in the form of 'responsibilities'.

Any negative interpretation of these powers has to be tempered once we
examine the wider context of discipline and control. Ideas parents have about their
children's developing public identities are largely generated from images parents
have of the public realm as a landscape populated by folk devils and hostile forces
(Miller, 1990). Rather than see this problem in terms of the narcissistic features of
the parent's self-identity – the projection of parental inadequacies on to the public
terrain (Seabrook, 1982) – parents tended to see these as concrete problems which
affected the quality of their children's development.

The problem of balancing the concept of adolescent autonomy with the
demands made on parents to exercise authority reappears. In respect to sanctioning

approaches, parents found it difficult to differentiate between authority and their children's individual responsibility. The distinction may be more clearly drawn by parents where the frame of reference is their children's public identities. But there is still the same problem of reconciling their children's demand for space outside of the home with a need ensure that this space is somehow circumscribed by parents.

We might at this stage draw on Donzelot's (1979) notion of the child's 'protected liberation', where children are granted a degree of freedom conditional on a parent's guarantee of safety. Parents attempted to provide a degree of protected liberation in two ways. First, parents supervised, wherever possible, their children's time outside of the home. Parental authority took more non-directive and sophisticated forms. Parents were able to avoid the visible assertion of their authority, vis-á-vis their adolescent children, by skilfully managing their children's spare time. In some instances this meant that parents knew where their children were and who they were with. In other instances parents managed their adolescent children's behaviour within the home through a form of regulated permissiveness: children were allowed to behave as immature adults within the confines of the private sphere of the home. Supervision gives parents a degree of authority over their children in the protection that parents offer children from their own naivety. This also gives parents some opportunity to steer their children in what they consider to be appropriate directions.

Secondly, parents made demands on the supervisory powers of the school. There is no necessary opposition between the home and the school. A few parents felt that they were under pressure to 'turn out' their children because of the superior judgmental powers of the school. But, in the main, the concerns that parents had about an uncivil society were more dominant. In a sense the parental frame of reference has shifted. Concerns about individual rights and parental primacy are displaced by public order themes of moral and physical control, issues which dominate the present cultural landscape. Parents were more interested in how the school could best be utilized in the successful management of their children's well-being outside of the home. Parents, when discussing their children's general moral and physical well-being, did not appear to subscribe to the views they expressed elsewhere that there was a fundamental distinction between their disciplinary responsibilities and the 'educational' role of the teacher.

When discussing the ways that their children were able to develop successful and secure relations with others outside of the home, parents couldn't afford the luxury of distancing themselves from the supervisory skills and expertise of the school. In the following chapter I reinforce this point when I turn to the ways that parents rely on the school to supervise the most public of 'private' concerns, their children's sexual identities.

Notes

1   The current debates over whether corporal punishment ought to be outlawed in Britain reflect deep concerns over physical child abuse. A lot of the academic concern goes back to early debates over the degree to which corporal punishment could be conceptualized,

at one end of a spectrum of domestic violence, as 'normal' violence. See Strauss, Gelles and Steinmetz (1980), Goode (1971) and, for a useful review of the literature, Parton (1985).

2 A 'clout' is a slight smack with the back of the hand.

3 See Wyness (1994) for a more detailed exposition of their work.

4 See Appendix 2 for more details.

5 As a consequence of these concerns, detention was no longer a part of St Mary's policy on school discipline.

6 The implications of this are discussed in the final chapter.

Chapter 5

Schooling and Sex Education

Introduction

In the previous chapter I outlined a dominant theme in parents' thinking about their child-rearing responsibilities: the need to underwrite their children's physical and moral welfare. Critics of welfare and schooling would tend to relate these ideas to an alleged loss of authority and a parallel increase in parental accountability. The school here is argued to be complicit in the opening up of parents to public scrutiny whilst denying them the means to satisfying demands made on them by a socially fragmented, sometimes hostile, public sphere.

I argued that, although parents may feel uncertain about the parameters of their responsibility in relation to both bringing up their adolescent children and the range of demands made on them from outside, the resultant anxiety did not always leave parents 'unskilled'. Control and supervision are critical elements within the parental sphere of influence (as they are for teachers in class). At a micro level of analysis, parents are able to account for how they adapt to range of conflicting external influences and accommodate any adolescent desires for independence through the concept of 'positive parental control'.

Furthermore, parents did not articulate the demands made on them in terms of some all-embracing notion of welfarism or child-centredness. Schools and teachers often took a lead in child supervision, a lead that was endorsed by the parents themselves.

In the following two chapters these arguments are further extended through an examination of the ways in which parents and teachers deal with the moral and physical welfare of their children from another angle, the teaching of sex education.

In Chapter 5, I address this thorny issue from the 'professionals' point of view. In the first part of this chapter I outline a discourse on sex education which parallels the debate over parental decline discussed in Chapter 1. The terms of the debate over sex education revolve around the institutional/natural, public/private oppositions with teachers again set up as irreconcilable moral and social influences. In the second and third parts of this chapter I examine the understandings teachers have of their relations with the home with respect to sex education and how this squares with their professional commitment to teaching sex education as part of the curriculum.

In Chapter 6, sex education is dealt with from the parental perspective. The first and second parts of the chapter deal with the perennial problem of where responsibility for sex education lies; firstly, between the home and the school and, secondly, in terms of the gender dimensions within the home. In the third part of the chapter I identify the reference points within which parents assert their children's right to a comprehensive sex education: the articulation of their own inadequate sex education as adolescents and a general perception of social change. The fourth part of the chapter provides a parental caveat in discussing the limits of formal sex talk at school. In the final part I sidestep the established terms of the debate. Sex education is normally defined as the deliberate and intentional handling of knowledge about sexual matters. As in Chapter 4, where I delineated the informal techniques of control, I argue that the routine business of bringing up children is suffused with everyday talk which contains implicit and explicit sexual codes that generate ideas and values. The notion of routine sex talk within the home is both an attempt to come to grips with the informal hidden aspects of moral supervision and a possible means by which parents resolve the problem of discharging their responsibilities as sex educators.

Sex Education and the Decline of Authority

In their review of the parenting of adolescents, the Rapoports remarked that one of the major areas that parents have trouble supervising is their children's sexuality (Rapoport, Rapoport and Strelitz, 1977, p. 199). The Rapoports paid particular attention to sexuality as a primary source of tension between parents and adolescent children. They argued that the development of the self is inextricably bound up with how adolescents perceive themselves as sexual beings which sharply contrasts with their parents' own more repressive image of their adolescence (1977, p. 299). This point seemed to have been anticipated by Davis a decade and a half earlier when he identified in parents an 'extraordinary preoccupation with the sex lives of their adolescent off-spring' (1962, p. 350). He argued that this was because:

> . . . our morality is sex-centred. The strength of the impulse which it seeks to control, the consequent stringency of its rules and the importance of reproductive institutions for society make sex so morally important that being moral and being sexually discreet are synonymous. (*ibid.*)

What has commonly been taken as a private 'preoccupation', has in recent years been articulated as a public or social problem in Britain.[1] Academic and public figures have expressed concern over the idea that parents are no longer assumed to be best suited to take 'care and control of the sexual life of [their] children' (Szasz, 1980, p. 153). Two developments are taken to be significant here: the sex education curriculum within schools and the identification of the late 1960s and early 1970s as a period of permissiveness in social and sexual manners. Sex education here tends to be conflated with permissiveness in that it is a part of a much more public discourse on sexuality. Sex education in schools is usually seen as an indication of the liberalizing of sexual mores. Talk about sex here is associated with the unfolding of what was previously repressed (Weeks, 1981, pp. 249–72; Foucault, 1976). Thus discussion about the sexual act within the classroom was taken as a transgression of moral taboos: discussions about sexual matters were argued to be legitimate only within the home.

But concern was not just expressed about what could appropriately be discussed in public; there was a concern that sex education would encourage immorality.

It would be possible to teach students the facts . . . about anatomy and physiology of the human organs, about contraception and abortion and so forth. But, as we have seen, sex educators do not want to impart informa-tion – they want to exert *influence*. (Szasz, 1980, p. 43, his emphasis)

Szasz was arguing that within a context of 'sexual liberation', the school couldn't be trusted to discuss the factual aspects of sex in neutral terms. Szasz was concerned with the implicit message of sex educators that the sexual act could be pleasurable in its own terms. Sex education did not aim to reaffirm a moral code about sexual behaviour. It was argued to foster ideas about sexual liberation.

The Longford Report took a similar line in documenting the emergence of a public discourse on sex. A chapter was devoted to the forms that this discourse took in schools. The report stated that there was no necessary link between pornography and sex education but that:

. . . the wrong sort of sex education can hardly fail to increase, the right sort to diminish, the appetite for pornography in childhood or later. (Longford Committee, 1972, p. 344)

Various school authorities and teenagers themselves were quoted in an attempt to emphasize public disapproval over the kinds of information being transmitted by the school. Publications such as the 'corrupt' *Little Red School Book* and the more scientific film by Dr Martin Cole, *Growing Up*, were produced as evidence of the kinds of media being used by educational authorities. Here the concern was over the content of sex education classes which were argued to either intentionally or unintentionally encourage adolescents to become sexually active. Thus, by merely presenting the facts on sex, educators were accused of corrupting school children.

'Moral corruption' in schools has been contested with reference to the discussion on homosexuality in schools. Two developments are important here. First, headlines such as 'Parents Fight Against Haringey's "Gay" Educational Policy' (*The Times*, 28.1.87, p. 16) and 'Baptist in Death Fast Over Council's Gay Policy' (*Times Education Supplement*, 23.1.87, p. 16) provided a context within which the govern-ment moved to proscribe the 'promotion' of homosexuality in schools through Clause 28 of Local Government Act, 1988.[2] A second concern was expressed over the AIDS campaign which surfaced around this period and reflected the concerns expressed in the Longford Report, that the description of both heterosexual and homosexual acts would encourage children to experiment with sex before they were judged to be 'naturally' ready.

Yet there is an important ambiguity here. Critics of sex education sometimes suggest that schools ought to err on the side of not teaching sex education for fear of pushing an unacceptable moral line. But Longford accepted the need for a restricted form of sex education. Longford, in fact, placed firm restrictions on which facts are acceptable for public consumption.

> Straight biological information, about the functioning of the human body [and] advice on the dangers of irresponsible sexual behaviour [are acceptable]: describing techniques of sexual congress [and] treating all sexual variations – from heterosexual intercourse, through masturbation to homosexual practices as simply different aspects of one reality [are not]. (Longford Committee, 1972, p. 350)

We get a quite different story here. If sex is taught in an acceptable fashion, that is, if sex is couched in terms of chastity and fidelity and heterosexuality, sex education becomes not only acceptable but mandatory.

More recently, the publication of the Government White Paper, *Health of the Nation* (HMSO, 1992), sets out an agenda for halving the teenage pregnancy rate in Britain. If we take this alongside a developing consensus over a sex education curriculum within the educational establishment (Reiss, 1993, p. 125), and the exigencies of the AIDS issue, there has been a perceptible shift towards a conditional pro-sex-education position.

The one consistent position adopted in the debates over sex education is the importance attributed to the parental role. If pragmatism over sex education in schools is the order of the day this may be a consequence of the general perception that parents have allegedly abdicated their responsibilities for sex education. What is argued to be at the root of the problem here is the Laschian notion of a general decline in parental authority. The Longford Report does make reference to the problems that parents face in introducing sexual morality to their children in that parents are quite often too embarrassed or lacking in technical know-how to discharge their natural responsibilities. But the emphasis is on sex education being a 'natural' parental responsibility. Parents were assumed to be able to solve the dual problem of public decency and sexual morality. Not only would sex be discussed within the appropriate sphere, it was assumed that parents would set the right moral guidelines within which their children would develop their sexuality in socially acceptable ways.

Like Lasch's (1977) critique of the state for its appropriation of parental moral functions, the report by implication is arguing for the return of these functions through giving parents back some powers of veto over what is taught in school.

> Sex education is primarily an affair for parents and must be emphasised by legislation which will ensure that no local authority will have the right to arrange programmes of sex education without the full consultation with parents, and any parent who objects to a sex education programme shall have the statutory right to withdraw his or her children from such a programme. (Longford Committee, 1972, pp. 356–7)

Teaching Assumptions about Parental Responsibility

Normative Responsibility

Almost all the guidance teachers had sex education responsibilities. They all stressed the importance of guidance and instruction in sexual matters. Dorothy Small, a teacher with thirty years' experience, outlined the context within which sex education assumed such importance.

> It [sex] is such a basic part of life. It's of tremendous concern to parents especially of girls. Relationships we make can make or mar our lives. Again coming back to society. There is so much in society . . . the people who are wanting the equality of the sexes. There are people who are maladjusted in some way and there seems to be . . . it might be statistical . . . there seems to be much more abduction, rape, violence against women . . . wife battering. Although you don't hear about it so much. Marriages not lasting as long as they used to. Children being left to pick up the pieces of their lives. So much now seems to hinge on the little act of sex. It leads to people having polarized views. People, on the one hand, saying of course they should know about contraception, responsibilities involved in relationships, shown what a condom is and told about abortion. On the other hand, there are those that say all this teaching of sex education just leads to promiscuity. It's telling them how to do things that they shouldn't know how to do.

It can be seen from the Table 5.1 that there is overwhelming teacher support for the view that the responsibility for guiding children through this tricky moral and social terrain lies with the parents. Dorothy Small again:

> Given the right kind of parent and the right kind of relationship, I would think that the parent was the ideal person to guide their children into the adult world as far as sex is concerned.

Dorothy Small is drawing on a normative notion of what parents ought to be doing. I want to concentrate for the moment on what this normative notion of parental responsibility might consist of. Although I will go on to argue that teachers claim a *de facto* responsibility for sex education, they do have a more detailed account about the de jure responsibility of parents.

There would appear to be three dimensions to the concept of parental responsibility suggested here. First, parents take responsibility for encouraging questions on the subject of sex:

> If a child is getting into difficulties with a sexual relationship where do they turn to? Unless the groundwork has been laid by the parent, they won't be able to turn to the parent. (Ian Howe)

Table 5.1: *Who ought to have responsibility for the teaching of sex education? (N = 20)*

Responsibility	Nos of Teachers
Parents	15
School	–
Joint	3
Don't Know	2
Total	20

This 'groundwork' takes place before the children reach adolescence, before the involvement of the secondary school. The teachers would expect parents to have said something to their children before they got involved in sex education as a more organized group activity outside of the domestic unit. The timing of sex education, especially for girls, was crucial according to Norah Bowles.

> It should be discussed at home when they are at primary school, especially with the girls. Parents should speak about it as long as the kids ask questions about it. I don't think you need to force it on them and say here are the facts of life. If they ask questions you give her straight answers. If you've got that kind of relationship developed early with your child then they'll ask you questions. If you haven't done this early enough, say from the age of five, then they're not going to ask you.[3]

Second, parents are to provide a minimum level of factual knowledge on sex. Interestingly, this contradicts a Weberian interpretation of sex education which would map the fact/value distinction on to the instrumental/affective axis. Thus, according to the teachers, parents are not charged solely with the task of drawing moral boundaries around the 'physiological facts of life' which are provided by 'instrumentalist public agents' such as teachers. Teachers only invoked this model as a last resort, that is, in circumstances where parents had abdicated responsibility for sex education.

> I like to see myself as somebody who talks about the moral aspect of it, the emotional side, rather than having to go through the actual facts of life. Having said that, growing up in the family is an implicitly moral thing and sex education comes through there. But I like to feel that when we're discussing generally certain aspects . . . you see a 15-year-old girl if she loves somebody should she go away with somebody etc . . . girls being responsible for their own bodies that's the kind of thing I'm happy discussing. I'm not very happy telling a class of kids about sexual intercourse. I really feel that that's up to the parents. (Anne Smart)

Third, parents sustain a dialogue with their children on sexual matters throughout their childhood; a period which would include some input from the schools. In this situation it is much easier for teachers to work with parents. Mary James from the Catholic school:

> I think there should be a mixture of both parental and school involvement. It's all right parents teaching on their own but they do need the backing of the priest, the church and the school. Parents need support because for the children what the parents say doesn't matter – they're old fashioned!

Parents' Involvement

Teachers measured the extent to which parents took any responsibility by drawing on a set of normative obligations parents had towards sex education. This assessment was based to a large extent on how children behaved in sex education classes. Ross Stewart was asked whether children ever mentioned things they had heard from parents. He claimed that he often used to ask pupils whether they had ever discussed sex with their parents.

> In general I sometimes say to a class, have any of your parents mentioned to you anything about sex? Any of them taken you aside and told you the birds and the bees? You'll get the heads all turning to see if some one has put a hand up. If one puts a hand up you might get two or three more following suit. But again you won't get them all honestly responding. I would say it's a fairly small percentage of pupils who have admitted to some parental sex education.

This approach was also used by Ian Howe who came to similar conclusions.

> I don't think they talk to their parents about sex. I've been teaching this for over sixteen years and that has remained constant, an inability for a whole host of reasons to talk to their parents about sex. I asked a group of twenty whether they had discussed sex with their parents. Probably no more than 25 per cent, mainly girls. Mainly related to menstruation.

Given the inhibiting nature of introductory classes in sex education teachers were unlikely to get an accurate reflection of parental involvement using this method. Teachers sensed that pupils received little information and guidance on sexual matters through the quality as well as the quantity of responses from children in class on a whole range of subjects on sex. In discussion with George Barry;

> MW: Would you prefer that the children came into the classroom better informed?

> GB: I think I would do if they came in with information from their parents, from people who are knowledgable. A lot of them come

> in with information which is picked up on street corners or from
> their big brothers or sister which is usually complete rubbish.

The assumption here is that parents either give sensible information or none at all.
Thus if pupils bring incorrect or unacceptable ideas into the classroom about sex,
teachers tend to take this as an indication of the power of more illegitimate sources
of sex education, such as peers (Lees, 1993, p. 202).

Some teachers saw difficulties with sex education as an indicator of more
general parental problems.

> We have to remember that all parents are not articulate enough. Therefore,
> we have a responsibility within the school to make our pupils leave school
> having been given the opportunity to hear and to discuss adult relations
> responsibly. We have a responsibility to make sure that they know about
> conception and contraception and the pitfalls and difficulties around that.
> Ideally that's part of the parents role but we've got to be aware that all
> parents aren't capable of playing that role and that we have to make sure
> that we fill that gap. (Dorothy Small)

Here there is the implicit reference to the problem parent and the idea of the 'best
interests of the child' ensures moral and social support from the school. Yet, lay
theories of problem parents also accommodated the specific nature of sex talk within
the home which affected otherwise 'normal' households. Explanations revolved
around the idea of a sex taboo which was expressed by the teachers in terms of
parental and, to a certain extent, adolescent embarrassment. Alice Tay expressed her
own embarrassment in trying to introduce sex to her adolescent son.

> All parents should teach their kids about sex but I can see that it's diffi-
> cult. Morality rubs off. I don't think you need to vocalize it. They pick
> up standards . . . what's acceptable. They're living in a house where they
> pick these things up. They'll pick up attitudes without having to sit down
> and thrash them out. I've found it difficult to engage my own son in con-
> versation. It's got to come naturally. Really its got to come from them.
> They've got to bring things up. A lot of parents find it embarrassing. A lot
> of the kids don't want to see their parents as sexual people. I think they
> can be a lot more open with an outsider.

Ian Dury had extensive ties with many of his pupils' parents through twenty-
three years of experience at the Catholic school. As well as knowing many of his
pupils on a personal basis, he had also taught many of their parents.

> I do think that children should know as much about sex as they possibly
> can. I know many people shy off from this – an awful lot of Catholics are
> shocked when it's mentioned. It's something all children are fascinated by.
> They better have the right attitudes and the right information, they might

as well get it from me as anybody else. But I'd prefer of course that parents do this, but parents don't do this. Mary [another guidance teacher] was doing a thing a few weeks ago when an outside agency comes in and does things with the girls. So I took all the boys. I told all the boys what the girls were away for and they all sat and listened while I went through the video the girls were seeing. I said really, ideally, your parents should tell you. You should ask your parents. But I know that many of you feel that you couldn't ask your parents and your parents wouldn't want to be asked. So you can ask me or your own guidance teacher.

This was also expressed by George Barry;

They [parents] are embarrassed about it. They find it difficult to get in to, to make a start on the subject, to introduce the subject, to set time aside and talk about it. So I think this is what they would have to do. They would have to get some time where it would crop up on television or something like that. I don't think they're very happy bringing the subject up.

Sexual Ignorance: Class and Gender

Teachers offered lay theories on sex education within the home by referring both to a model of the absent parent and a sex taboo within the home. Again, as in the case of problem pupils, teachers were less likely to attribute a class dimension to these problems.

These figures in Table 5.2 are based on the impression that teachers had from their own experiences. What teachers were claiming here was that the kind of training they had received, the kinds of close contacts they had with the children in conducting classes and discussion groups on sex, and the kinds of values they brought to the teaching process didn't lead them to think that there was a systematic enough difference in quality and quantity of sex education taught and discussed in families along social class lines. Sixty-five per cent of the teachers claimed that social class was not a significant factor. Of the minority that were able to assess the extent to which their pupils had received sex education in class terms, most argued that working-class children were more knowledgable. It may be that these children were more street wise and therefore more likely to pick up sex education outside of the home and the school. This may help explain the following statement by Anne Smart.

. . . some of the ones from the poorer backgrounds had very strong views about things; very keen to make points about a woman's role or whatever. The better off ones were slightly more reserved in a sense in discussing it.

Yet, when giving reasons for why they thought working-class children had more knowledge of sex, teachers mentioned the children's home circumstances. Ian Howe argued that:

Table 5.2: *The extent to which social class features in teachers' perceptions of sex education within the home (N = 20)*

Teachers' Perceptions	Nos of Teachers
Social class had no significance	13
Working-class children had more knowledge than middle-class children	5
Middle-class children had more knowledge than working-class children	2

> Working-class children are more likely to have uncles or aunties or broth-
> ers or sisters who become parents at an earlier age. I think the young mar-
> ried relative will probably talk about looking after a young child.

In contrast, teachers tended to recognize differences within families along more
familiar sociological lines. In looking more specifically at which parent and which
child was having particular difficulties, the teachers tended to focus on both father
and son (Lees, 1993, p. 201). This was partially brought out in the discussion on
the significance of social class, in that several teachers stated that it was sex rather
than class which was far more significant, but also more substantively when asked
about gender differences.

The behaviour and general dispositions of girls were seen to be different from
that of boys in the sex education classes. A recurring theme was that girls were more
sensitive and mature than boys in sex education classes.

> Girls are more mature, more prepared to take the issue seriously. When
> emotions and relations are discussed, girls are always keener, more articu-
> late. In general boys are more embarrassed, less keen to discuss their per-
> sonal feelings. They cover this up by joking and fooling around. (Joan Leslie)

According to the teachers, this difference in behaviour would seem to have some
of its roots in the kinds of ways boys and girls were treated as future sexual beings
within the home by their parents. When asked about the role they thought parents
played in general, George Barry said:

> I think a lot of them are doing very little . . . giving the youngsters little
> information, especially the boys. I think the girls are a wee bit more aware
> now. I think mainly their mums do talk to them about it. But I would say
> in the main boys don't get a lot. With girls there is occasion. It's often
> there for them to speak and get some information. (George Barry)

The 'occasion' that George Barry was referring to was the more marked physiological
developments of girls than boys. Ruth Smith was asked whether she thought her
pupils had received sex education from their parents.

Some of them seem to, but a lot of them don't. They get embarrassed. From what the kids say the boys might talk to their dads a bit but I don't think they discuss an awful lot with each other. There's not an awful lot of communication between them. The girls might say a bit more to their mums about certain things, periods, probably not actual sex. (Ruth Smith)

The Parental Veto

The parental veto over sex education in schools is a key feature of the 1993 Education Act. In one sense, the act reinforces the efforts of pastoral and guidance teachers to provide a coherent and organized package of sex education classes because it defines sex education as a compulsory component of the curriculum.[4] Yet, the Act also appears to undermine these efforts in that it strengthens the rights of parents to exclude their children from this component of the curriculum. Although teachers tended to articulate these rights in terms of parental primacy, as I have argued earlier they were also guided by a professional commitment to their pupils, commonly expressed as 'educational needs' or the 'best interests of the child'. The parental veto might be seen as an explicit expression of parental primacy. It might also be seen as a form of educational intervention converging on the notion of the 'over ambitious' or 'pushy' parent discussed in Chapter 3.

Although this research predates the Act, the parental veto was crucially important to the teachers. First, the schools taught sex as part of a broader social or health curriculum. All of the schools made some form of formal statement about their children receiving a social or health education curriculum as a compulsory, unassessed aspect of their child's education. Yet the formal documentation sent to parents at the beginning of the academic year rarely gave more detailed information on what social education consisted of: 'sex education' was not explicitly referred to. The one exception was the Catholic school where it was mentioned as an aspect of social and religious education.[5] A form of parental veto existed in this school because it included the right of parents to withdraw their children from religious education in its Catholic form. (There was a small minority of non-Catholic children.) Thus, in theory, some non-Catholic children could miss out on the sex education that was taught within the religious curriculum. In the other schools, parents tended to be informed by letter that sex education was going to be discussed as part of social education, but the burden was very much on the parents to question the legitimacy of this. Parents were never actively encouraged to exclude their children from sex education classes.

Second, the parental veto highlighted a tension between the moral and social ideals of the school and professional practice. In this chapter, I have identified the importance teachers placed on parents having a formative influence on their children's sex education. The parent was seen as the ideal and 'natural' source of information and guidance on sexual matters. But the degree to which teachers believed that parents neglected this area of their responsibility and the extent to which parents supported the role of the school, was a sufficient reason for the school to take responsibility for sex education. Any attempt to undermine this approach was interpreted by the schools as an intrusion. As I have argued, in relation to parent power this was a more general problem. The problem was not that parents actively undermined the professional *raison d'être* of teachers, it was that a veto had to provide the means whereby parents had the power to intervene in the education process. This was summed up by Ruth Smith. She was asked whether she ever discussed sex education with parents.

> If they [the parents] bring it up I would. A while back we used to send a letter allowing them to opt out. But now we don't do that. I think there's information in the school book that they all get and they're all told that sex education is taught. If they want to opt out I dare say they can but we don't make it easy for them.

This was not simply a question of the school setting up barriers of 'social enclosure'. There was an important teaching reason for discouraging parents from opting out. Ruth Smith continued:

> I think if a child has to sit in another room when sex education is being taught, the other children know. It puts that child in a difficult situation.

The emphasis was on the problems this created for children that were excluded from normal classroom activities. From the child's point of view there is probably a degree of stigmatizing going on, a process of which guidance teachers were only too aware and eager to avoid.

Although a parental veto would have the potential for creating problems for teachers, in practice very few parents tried to withdraw their children from sex education classes. As we shall see in the following chapter, parents placed a high priority on sex education in schools.

Problems with the parental veto were articulated by the teachers from Boreston in terms of an ethnic dimension. Boreston had a significant minority of Asian children (17 per cent). Parents, particularly of muslim girls, were more likely to insist that other arrangements be made (Lees, 1993, p. 210). In the other schools, most of the teachers interviewed were usually able to mention one or two cases where parents had objected to sex education on religious or cultural grounds, but these were always recounted as exceptions. This was borne out by the parents interviewed. None of them ever brought up the subject of sex education at parents' meetings.

Where contact was more consistently and more formally made by the school was in the area of health education, particularly over the AIDS issue. All schools were directed by the education department to discuss in detail the dangers of the AIDS virus. Head teachers had to write to every parent informing them of the nature and extent of the information that was being discussed in the classrooms. Some of the schools also invited parents to view the video that was going to be shown to their children in class. Thus, the AIDS issue seemed to have galvanized the schools into taking more action as regards to informing parents.

The Professional Sex Educator

Teachers' conduct in class is a crucial indicator of their sense of professionalism. In Chapter 2 I outlined the different forms this can take in routine classroom situations. Sex education classes threaten this professionalism: partly because it is a non-assessed and in many ways non-curricular teaching activity and thus does not fit into the dominant teaching paradigm; and, partly because it opens the teacher up to a range of moral and social pressures for which their professional training does not prepare them. Ross Stewart felt that male teachers were at a disadvantage discussing sex with female pupils.[6]

> I don't know if I'm more sensitive to the way girls react because I'm a male teacher. I try and think that I'm professional enough to do my job, but I still have inhibitions. For example with a group of boys I'll more readily use all the names that are used for a penis. Whereas I find myself a little bit inhibited about saying 'right girls, the vagina. Now tell me what are all the names?' It's easier when it's all boys together.

There were similar problems for the two female guidance teachers at Stenhouse. For Ruth Smith:

> Vocabulary can be a problem. I'm not very happy with the swear words I have to say, but apart from that I'm okay. Sometimes I ask them what sort of words they use. One of the techniques recommended was to brainstorm at the beginning and use all the words. Stick them all up on the board and get it out of the way. I couldn't quite bring myself to do that.

In Norah Bowles' case:

> In biology it was quite easy, it's in biological terms. I'm quite comfortable with them. I tend not to go red. Sometimes you get a few giggles but not always because they have to try and remember it all. I wasn't too comfortable with social education which I taught for the first time. It became a more personal thing. Not using biological terms. The children wanted to know the nitty gritty. I questioned the class and I was asking myself what have I let myself in for? I tend to go red very easily. It's a thing I never manage to control. I wasn't comfortable with the slang words for the genitalia.

The problems were most acutely felt at St Mary's, over the issue of AIDS. The teachers interviewed from this school stressed the importance of discussing morality within the context of the Catholic doctrine. Bill Short, the assistant head, was asked about discussion on AIDS within the school.

> Catholic teaching in that area is quite clear. The church sees it going against nature. It's a natural product of intercourse within a loving marriage.

> Homosexuality in that context is simply an aberration. We can be sympa-
> thetic to homosexuals who feel that way . . . are attracted to their own sex
> but the activity is not acceptable.

Concerns here were more related to their own religious beliefs and the more generalized expectations that a Catholic school couldn't be seen to condone contraception, no matter how rationally defensible the campaign was. Because there was little
pressure from within the school to include it within the sex education curriculum
this wasn't seen as a problem for the teachers. They simply didn't discuss AIDS.
Mary James became very angry when the subject of AIDS was brought up.

> We were just suddenly issued with a package which I only saw for the first
> time last term. I hadn't had time to look at it. I took it along to a class
> and started on it and I was really disgusted. I took it back to the AHT
> [assistant head teacher] and said I am not prepared to dish that out to the
> children. I felt it was just putting ideas into the children's heads on homo-
> sexuality, explicitly detailing how to go about it. To me that is putting
> ideas into children's heads. Some of the children had never heard of such
> a thing. It was quite disgusting telling them how to use condoms, telling
> them what homosexuals do. I don't think there's any need for children to
> be bombarded with this stuff at this age. I refused to teach it. I don't feel
> competent to dish that out.

Finally, teachers sometimes had to face the problem of challenges to their
authority from what Liz Sim called 'breakaway groups'. Willis (1977) has outlined
the ways that a group of problem pupils skilfully exploit the fact that teachers are
in a physical minority in class. But whereas the 'lads' were exploiting the unfairness
of the pupil–teacher exchange in Willis' study, teachers here were referring to the
sensitive nature of the curriculum. The embarrassment of the child can be sub-
merged within the pupil group in sex education classes. This leaves the teacher in
a more vulnerable position because the very nature of sex education does not lend
itself to being separated from the personal background of the teacher. The lack of
professionalism here can on occasion be exploited by the pupil by testing out the
teacher. Andy Hargreaves (1994, p. 150) refers to the ways that teachers conceal
their personal lives from 'public' consumption by 'constructing a persona of (professional) perfectionism'. This is particularly pertinent in relation to sex education.
As one teacher asserted in response to a question on the best way of tackling sex
education, the teacher has to be:

> . . . willing not to be embarrassed, that's the main thing. Teenagers being
> teenagers, they'll try and embarrass you because it's a way of handling their
> own embarrassment. Whenever the subject comes up there's usually some
> joke or smutty comment . . . they'll project their own embarrassment on to
> somebody else. You have to be totally unembarrassable or pretend to be.

Discussions over teaching practice reveal that sex education cannot be easily incorporated within a traditional curricular framework with the same degree of professional confidence as other subjects. Where a school is bound by a particularly strong moral code or ethos, such as St Mary's, the introduction of certain sexual issues, can quite easily be interpreted as departing from what can be safely contained within the school's moral parameters. The AIDS issue seems to serve as one example of this. In another sense, the AIDS issue acted as a useful medium through which teachers were able to gauge levels of awareness and opinion on sexual morality. Dorothy Small introduced AIDS to a group of 15 year olds and was surprised at their lack of knowledge.

> In the fourth year we were talking about homosexuality. The kids had no real idea what this was. Some of the kids were genuinely upset about the practice of homosexuality. I wondered then whether I should be doing this or let somebody else.

Vivien Willis was asked whether she found sex education more difficult because of the AIDS issue.

> No, it's made it easier, from the point of view of discussion. People are aware of the facts. You don't have to teach so many facts nowadays.

Interestingly, these statements seem to contradict each other. But they do serve to emphasize the way in which teachers can measure levels of knowledge about sexual matters. Even more interesting were the connections that some of the teachers were able to make about the level of understanding within the classroom and the kinds of verbal symbols that circulated within the household. Here we also pick up on the changing conception of childhood, this time from the teacher's perspective.

> I've noticed that they use the word 'celibacy' which I wouldn't have expected children to know the meaning of. It's been picked up from parents. The idea that no sex before marriage or no sex until a stable relationship is very much more to the fore now. AIDS has had the spin off of a lot of discussion on morality and probably a lot more discussion with parents on morality because it's in the living room now, on television. Parents have been helped to talk more openly with their children. (Vivien Willis)

Conclusion

The teachers, as I discussed in Chapter 3, were working with the products of the labours of others, no matter how inadequate they might have thought the results were. Most of the teachers were pragmatic enough to adjust their everyday working commitments to what they thought parents had been doing with their children with regards to sex instruction.

Much of the current political and moral debate over the universalistic nature of the post-war welfare system revolves around lack of differentiation between those who need and those who don't need material and educational support from the state (Friedman, 1962; Levitas, 1986; Mishra, 1984). Whether or not the welfare state undermines the educational functions of parents who are quite capable of taking responsibility for the sex education of their children, teachers do still see themselves as having a responsibility to teach sex education to all pupils. With the recent advent of AIDS, and with the exception of teachers from St Mary's, teachers tend to err on the side of too much information and advice on sex. The assumptions teachers have about the role of parents here are always conditioned by this generalized assessment. Vivien Willis summed up this pragmatic approach best:

> Sometimes parents have asked about what's in the sex education pro-
> gramme, not often though. I think they're quite happy. They don't want
> us to duck any issues because some of these pupils are going to leave at
> 16 and this'll be the last enclosed area for discussion that everybody will
> be in. They're going out into the world and they're going to be bombarded
> with lots of media ideas, and lots of peer group ideas. They're not going
> to have a space, many of them, to think their ideas through. For some, sex
> education is too soon, that's the trouble. That's just one of these things.
> It's better it's done than not at all.

Notes

1 Although sex education would appear to be a fundamental aspect of socialization in most societies, it is less of a public issue in some countries. According to Goldman and Goldman (1982, p. 70), Sweden has a more open approach to 'discussions on sex' and a public consensus over sex education in schools. Holland is also used as a reference point for more enlightened attempts at introducing sex education (Wallace, 1993).

2 This was later effectively rescinded. School governors who are outside local government jurisdiction had the power to determine sex education in schools (Sex Education Forum, 1988).

3 I will discuss the reference to gender later in chapter.

4 Research which pre-dates the act suggests that around 20 per cent of schools had no sex education policy (Stears and Clift, 1991).

5 Sex education here is defined as an 'extension of the religious and social education programme' in *St Mary's: Parent Guide*, 1988, p. 11.

6 This wasn't a problem at St Mary's as classes were single sex and female teachers had sole responsibility for the girls.

Chapter 6

Parents and Sex Talk within the Home and School

Parental Perception and the Sex Taboo

In this chapter I discuss the importance of sex education by directly addressing the decline thesis' notion that teachers undermine a parent's capacity to introduce sex education within the home. Table 6.1 suggests that parents do not share the same fears as the decline theorists' concerns over sex education in school.

Only five parents asserted that parents had more responsibility than the school. Alice Roper was an exceptional case in arguing for sole responsibility:

MW: What do you think about the school discussing sex in terms of health and moral issues?

AR: Well, I think it's the parents' job to do that rather than the schools. I really think, especially moral attitudes. It has to come from the parents. You have to show them moral values.

MW: Some people are quite happy with the school taking a big part in this.

AR: No I think it's up to the parents to teach right from wrong, what's acceptable and what's unacceptable.

MW: Why parents?

AR: Who knows their children best? Also they've got to live in the real world, not an ideal version which they get from school.

Almost all parents asserted the importance of the role of the school in discussing sex with their children. In contrast to the teachers, Table 6.1 shows that 30 per cent of all parents interviewed thought that teachers were best placed to take responsibility for sex education. This at least, in part, reflects the embarrassment parents felt in discussing sex with their children as shown in Table 6.2.

Table 6.1 would appear to point to a more general trend, that a majority of parents from both social classes thought teachers were at least as well qualified as

Table 6.1: *Parental opinion on who ought to have ultimate responsibility for sex education, by social class (N = 44)*

Opinion	Middle class	Working class	Total
Parents	3 (12.5)	2 (10)	5 (11)
School	5 (21)	8 (40)	13 (30)
Joint	16 (66.5)	10 (50)	26 (59)
Total	24	20	44

* Figures in brackets refer to percentages of parents within each social class category.

Table 6.2: *Parents who expressed embarrassment when discussing sex with their children, by social class (N = 44)*

Feeling	Middle class	Working class	Total
Embarrassed	8 (33)	9 (45)	17 (39)
Not Embarrassed	16 (67)	11 (55)	27 (61)

* Figures with brackets refer to percentages of parents with each social class category.

they were. Teachers had two important functions in this respect. First, the teacher played a crucial outside role as the stranger in introducing sex to their children, whereas parents lacked the psychological and moral space within which to discuss sex with their children. Parents, like the teachers, were implicitly drawing on some notion of a sex taboo in invoking the role of the stranger.

In the previous chapter, it was shown that teachers held the view that sex education was a parental responsibility. Parents here were reflecting a contrary set of assumptions about discussing sex within the home. Farrell (1978, p. 6) quotes Gagnon and Simon, in arguing that:

> learning about sex in our society is learning about guilt; conversely learning how to manage sexuality constitutes learning how to manage guilt.

Gagnon and Simon point to a sex taboo which is general to the whole society. Parsons (1965) in his analysis of sex within the family, however, more specifically relates this to a prohibition on incest. More recently the issue of child sex abuse has highlighted problems 'managing sexuality' within the home (La Fontaine, 1990). If we refer back to Harris' (1983) version of the decline thesis, a tension is articulated between a parental responsibility as a given moral absolute and a parent's ability to control and discipline their children. Sex education offers an interesting theoretical parallel in that the decline thesis suggests that parents have ultimate responsibility for discussing sexual matters with their children. Yet the decline thesis says little about how parents are simultaneously deprived of the ability to discharge this responsibility because of a set of countervailing values which come under the general rubric of a sex taboo. There would appear to be a tension that parents need to deal with; between the normative idea that parents ought to have responsibility for the moral education of their children where their future sexual identities are crucial, and the generalized problem about talking about sex. If we focus more on the latter, criticisms of the school would seem to be misplaced. The skills and training of the guidance teacher may very well off-set the personal discomfort experienced by parents when discussing sex. This directly conflicts with more conservative opinion on the advantages that the privacy of the home has for discussing issues such as sex. For the parents the teacher plays a legitimate role as an outsider in resolving the tension which revolves around biological and emotional closeness and sexual distance which were discussed earlier. When asked whether she ever discussed sex with her children Betty Deary, a part-time cleaner, replied

> Billy [her son] has never once really said anything . . . with Jean [daughter] I've spoken a wee bit, but Billy gets awfy embarrassed. He gets embarrassed when you try tae explain what they were saying on the television.

When asked if she had ever discussed the moral side of sex she replied, 'With Billy I feel my face goes as red as his'. Parental embarrassment was more specifically referred to by David Roper, an unemployed sales assistant. When asked if there was anything he was uncomfortable discussing with his children, he said:

> I imagine I'm fairly typical because I break out in a cold sweat when I have to talk about sex. Probably my upbringing. Sex was never discussed in my house with my parents.

Similarly, Frank Rodgers, a social worker, replied:

MW: Do you find sex difficult to discuss?

FR: There are easier subjects to discuss, things we'd prefer the teacher to bring up.

MW: Why?

FR: Because of the subject . . . people are embarrassed, naturally shy etc. I think if I taught it I'd die of embarrassment.

As well as parents feeling uncomfortable with sex education, they also felt unqualified. The teacher was not only someone that the parents trusted, but someone who was trained to discuss sex education. The teacher acted as an informed legitimate stranger.

Although class difference doesn't hold in terms of the numbers of parents who advocated the school when discussing the technical advantages the school has over the parent, there is an interesting difference in response.[1] This can be exemplified by comparing two discussions. The first was with John White; a plumber.

MW: How do you feel about the school teaching sex education?

JW: All right. It's better that they listen to a stranger telling them than us. We've no books on it or anything so I suppose they can put it in better words and the kids will understand it better than what we could.

MW: What about the moral aspects?

JW: Aye it's better for the school to talk about it.

MW: Why?

JW: It is easier for strangers to discuss it than parents. They'll no' take it all in and maybe laugh with parents. Whereas wie' strangers they'll take it in better.

MW: Some people say it's no business of the school?

JW: No, no. I'm a great believer in everyone to their own trade. The teacher knows better about teaching than I do. If I knew as much as a teacher I'd be a teacher, and no' a plumber, know what I mean.

MW: A recent thing they're saying in some quarters is that it was the parents' responsibility then and it still should be.

JW: I'm quite happy that the school does it because I think with the school doing it and you've got them all as a unit, twenty or thirty o' them au the gither, they could treat it more openly. They may get a wee snigger at the start of it in the first or second lesson, but it'll be treated as a subject after that and they can all sit and discuss it quite seriously I'd imagine.

Although broadly in agreement with this approach, George Terry, a photographer with the Civil Service, offered a slightly different version:

MW: Have you ever thought about taking your sons aside?

GT: Frequently, but I just don't know where to start.

MW: You're having difficulties?

GT: I would find it difficult because I wouldn't want to confuse them. If I started I'd probably give them too much information. This is becoming less of a problem the older they get. When they are sort of nine I'd probably give them too much. For this reason I'd certainly prefer the school. They're better at it than I am. They've got more knowledge as to what children can absorb.

MW: What about the moral aspects?

GT: A great minefield. I'm quite happy for it to be dealt with in the school. I don't want to sound complacent but it's an area where I think the school is better.

This class difference is interesting because although these examples would suggest that there is some credence to the claim that the middle class has greater access to a body of technical knowledge, this does not automatically mean that middle-class parents can apply this knowledge with any great confidence. George Terry, for example, acknowledges the superior skills of the school in that teachers knew how to handle this knowledge. Teachers knew better than parents when to introduce information on sex to children. Both middle-class and working-class parents invoked the bring them up/educate them dichotomy here again, with sex education being defined in mainly educational terms. But working-class parents defer to the school because of their general educational expertise. Middle-class parents, on the other hand, see the school as having more specific knowledgable advantages than themselves. In these terms teachers have more specific educational advantages over parents.

If we refer back to Table 6.1 a majority of parents, (59 per cent), mentioned a division of responsibility between the home and the school.[2] Although more middle-class than working-class parents invoked a form of division of responsibility, there was no social class difference in the ways in which teachers and parents ought to be working together. Some parents found it easier to tackle the questions they were asked by their children after the school had been involved. Like the previous section, parents here were expressing a confidence in the schools in their ability to introduce sex formally. For many parents this meant minimizing the possibility that their children would be asking inappropriate questions or making comments picked up outside the home and the school. In contradiction to the claims made by the teachers about parents setting the agenda, parents were asserting that the school was laying the factual ground upon which parents would be able to confidently express their opinions on sex. When she was asked about the extent to which she had discussed sex with her children, June Wilkins, a part-time cleaner, replied:

I think it would probably be easier after the school's done it because then again they [the children] come and ask you the questions . . . I mean teachers are just as qualified as me to teach it.

Sex, then, can be introduced in a professional manner within the classroom. This would provoke the child into initiating the discussion at home as the knowledge picked up in the classroom is brought home to the parents for confirmation and clarification. Jim Short, a self-employed builder, indicated the problem of parental embarrassment in relation to the factual aspects of sex education but qualified the role of the school:

I think they [the school] have to discuss it now. It's always going to be an embarrassing thing for parents. I think the schools can put it over in a very formal way. The school is the place for it, yes.

117

When asked about the moral dimension, he summed this up by saying: 'teaching morals is the parents' job, sex should be taught by the schools'. Sex education for Jim Short, then, was the province of the schools because sex education was defined in more factual terms.

The Davies, through their strongly held Christian convictions, were both concerned about the kinds of values that were being discussed within the school. Ian Davies had:

> . . . no fundamental objections. The physical side has got to be discussed ethically and morally. Not so much in the vague sense of just man and woman, but husband and wife. I believe the nature of the relationship should be discussed.

Doubts about whether the school would be able to do this were expressed by Alice Davies.

> I'm happy with them dealing with the physiological aspect. I don't know in this day and age that I expect them to take a moral stance because I know that my moral stance is not going to be the same as somebody else. So how can the school take an absolute straight moral stance?

The Davies were pointing to one of the difficulties that runs through much of the debates on sex education; the necessity of talking about the physiological side of sex in a moral way which implicitly means the school taking on board some of the moral responsibilities that traditionally parents are supposed to have had. Ian Davies again:

> In terms of acquiring and imparting knowledge, yes, because that's their business. From an ethical point of view they probably have to put across a standard moral line. To what extent they can modify that to include their own viewpoints, I don't know. It's an area that up until you asked me about it I'm not one hundred per cent sure where the obligation lies in terms of how they direct the ethical issue.

Sex Education: A Collective Parental Responsibility?

Parents often talked about parenting as a collective responsibility in relation to sex education. Yet, it became clear as the interviews progressed that, following the teachers, parents were articulating important differences in the way in which they and their spouses attempted to discuss sex with their children. The analysis at this point is restricted to the more formal aspects of sex education. Tables 6.3 and 6.4 give a fairly crude shape to the concept of collective responsibility in that parents are able to state more or less who does what with regards to the formal aspects of sex. The lines drawn between the categories are by no means mutually exclusive in that although the 'mother only' category meant that mothers had a major role in

Table 6.3: *Division of responsibility for sex education within the home, by social class*
(N = 22)

Responsibility	Middle class	Working class	Total
Joint	6	5	11 (50)
Mother only	6	2	8 (36)
No Sex Education	–	3	3 (14)
Total	12	10	22

* Figures in brackets refer to percentages of parents within each social class category.

sex education within the home, on occasions fathers did become more involved. Table 6.3 suggests that social class might *not* tell us much about the way that parents divide up the responsibility for broaching the subject of sex with their children. However, the same table does suggest that social class might be important in differentiating *between* households where sex was discussed and households where sex was not discussed.

If we turn to Table 6.4 the three working-class couples who had not attempted to discuss sex were parents with boys only. The figures are insufficient to make the connection between numbers of parents who had discussed sex with their children and the gender of their children, but some parents did articulate important differences between how their sons and daughters would be treated. At one end of the spectrum of parental opinion was Dave Deary who stated that:

Sex isn't something that's discussed much here. I think my wife will tell the girl. Girls need more enlightenment than boys. Well that's ma opinion, anyway. There again, I'm getting back to the old-fashioned ways.

Dave Deary's views were atypical in that he was the only parent who completely rejected 'modern methods' of child rearing. But parents were articulating some sense of difference between how boys and girls ought to be treated with regards to sex education. This difference was discussed by Christine Terry who had discussed sex with her three sons. When asked to comment on the controversial nature of sex education she said: 'It isn't anything I worry about. I might if I had girls.' When asked why, she admitted: 'I don't know really. I suppose girls get into more scrapes than boys.'

More generally, this difference was brought out through the more gendered pattern of parenting. Table 6.4 appears to reflect the findings of Allen (1987), Measor (1989) and Prendergast and Prout (1989). Teenagers and parents in the Allen study were asked which parent tended to discuss sex within the home. The teenagers claimed that 72 per cent of fathers and 43 per cent of mothers said nothing. This of course was not corroborated by the parents (we would expect there to be some difference in response between the recipient and donor of sex education) with 37 per cent of fathers and 21 per cent of mothers claiming not to have discussed sex (Allen, 1987, pp. 84–7).

The important point to be made here is that, although there was no consensus as to whether both boys and girls required the same level of sex education, mothers

Table 6.4: Division of Responsibility for sex education within the home, by sex of children (N = 22)

Responsibility	Both	Girls only	Boys only	Total
Joint	5	–	3	8 (36)
Mother only	5	3	3	11 (50)
No Sex Education	–	–	3	3 (14)
Total	10	3	9	22

* Figures in brackets refer to percentages of parents within each social class category.

had more responsibility. Mothers took exclusive responsibility for their daughters. Both parents saw this as natural given the greater insights and experiences of mothers in the development of female sexuality. Mother–daughter relationships here take on an acutely privatized form with fathers having little or no direct input. This was brought out by Ian Davies:

> There have been no open discussions about sex. I'm not privy to the extent of her discussions with my wife. From time to time my wife will go up and say good night and they'll get into discussions. I hear about a discussion having taken place but not all the ins and outs.

The exclusion from the mother–daughter relationship didn't always mean that the father had no power or influence over matters. Farrell argued that fathers backed up their spouses' 'responsibility for sex education by "allowing mothers to do most of the informing" (1978, p. 99). Tom Mctear was able to keep an eye on his daughter indirectly through his wife who would frequently report back to him:

> Personally, I would find it difficult to start the conversation, just actually broaching the subject. But fortunately I have a good wife in that respect. She finds out all these wee things and talks them through especially with the lassie. She'll come to me and she'll say, she'll tell me what's going on. That way I'm no' in the dark. I know what's happening. It doesn't need me sticking my nose in. At least I can watch and see what's happening.

If we turn to the sex education of sons there isn't an equivalent degree of paternal responsibility. Although there was some expectation that fathers would be more involved, there certainly was not the same close-knit intimacy between fathers and sons which excluded mothers. For some mothers there was an acute awareness of what their husbands ought to be doing. In five out of the eleven relevant households with sons there was a tension between the fathers' reticence to take their sons aside and their wives inevitable acceptance of this through having to take on a responsibility which they felt ought to lie with the father. June Wilkins, although taking responsibility, was still actively pushing her husband to do more.

> I must admit when even when he's talking to me, I'd much rather he asked his dad. You know, but he won't for some reason. He usually comes to

me. There are some things that are best coming from a man. He's a big boy now. I find it slightly embarrassing, I must admit.

Kathleen Adams was in the process of discussing the moral aspects with her daughter and was hoping that her husband would take responsibility for her son:

It's about time Jim was told and my husband says he's going to do it. He hasn't got round to it yet but he's got a book to help him.

Although he claimed to do 'an awful lot of pontificating from [his] soap box', George Adams was having problems in getting round to discussing sex directly with his son. There was a strong desire on the part of both the Adams that Jim would be taken aside within the next few months and there was frequent mention of the book that George had bought for the job.

In summary, we might say that fathers had most difficulty in reconciling their parental obligations with sustained and consistent action, and this forced mothers to play the major and, in some cases, sole role as sex educator within the home.

Repeating the Mistakes of the Past?

In Chapter 4, the early adolescent experiences of parents were shown to be an important component of the normative expectations of parents. This was also the case in relation to sex education. Most of the parents were aged between thirty-six and forty-four.[3] They were therefore growing up in the late 1950s and early to mid-1960s; adolescence falling for many during the period before the so-called 'permissive era'. Parents when asked to go back twenty and thirty years were often only able to give very impressionistic answers.[4] Yet the figures from Tables 6.5 and 6.6 would appear to agree with the figures in Allen's study in that parents held their own sex education in 'very low esteem' (1987, p. 107).

According to Table 6.6 only eight parents had received any sex education; a majority had received it at school. Jean Robbie, one of the parents who had received some sex education:

Going back to when I was younger we didn't talk about it in our home. Your mum and dad didn't tell you about anything. At school you were shown films but you didn't actually talk to your mum and dad about it. There was always a sort of barrier when talking about sex.

There were those like the Ropers who were critical of the current sex education teaching in school (See p. 201). They were also critical of the form that sex education took when they were at school. Alice Roper emphasized the problems the school had in dealing with the physiological aspects of sex. For her sex education was

. . . taught very badly . . . a mixed class . . . with an embarrassed teacher showing slides and photographs. I picked up half of it wrong . . . just the

Table 6.5: *Parents' own sex education, by sex of parent (N = 44)*

Sex education?	Father	Mother	Total
Had sex education from parents	1 (5)	2 (9)	3 (7)
Had sex education from school	2 (9)	3 (14)	5 (11)
No sex education	17 (77)	12 (54)	29 (66)
No response	2 (9)	5 (23)	7 (16)
Total	22	22	44

* Figures in brackets without percentage marks refer to percentages within the social class category.

Table 6.6: *Parents' own sex education, by social class (N = 44)*

Sex education?	Middle class	Working class	Total
Had sex education from parents	3 (12.5)	–	3 (7)
Had sex education from school	3 (12.5)	2 (10)	5 (11)
No sex education	14 (58)	15 (75)	29 (66)
No response	4 (17)	3 (15)	7 (16)
Total	24	20	44

* Figures in brackets without percentage marks refer to percentages within the social class category.

mechanics. More a biology lesson rather than sex education. It was just uncomfortable for everybody involved.

This was reiterated by her husband:

My own sex education at school just wasn't worth having . . . usually a 50-year-old spinster or bachelor. It was all the birds and bees, pollen and fish and eggs and things like that.

Iris Alison rather humourously describes the lengths to which other authority figures went to ensure that sex was discussed only in the most discreet and privatized of circumstances.

I went to a convent school and we had a book. My kids all laugh at this. It was in a sealed brown envelope and it was to be given to your parents for their approval first.

Table 6.6 illustrates a slight social class difference but the more significant point to be made here is that well over half of middle-class parents and three-quarters of working-class parents had received no sex education. As expected more mothers than fathers received sex education, yet there were interesting differences in the

quality of responses. Within the group of parents who had received no sex education, five fathers claimed to have been influenced by external sources. These fathers
tended to invoke the public sphere in vaguer, more evocative terms. Three of the
fathers defined their sources around the peer group with the 'gents toilets' (George
Wilson), 'behind the gym' (Richard Stone) and 'dirty magazines' (Bob Alison)
figuring as focal points for their 'education'. For John White and Dave Deary, sex
education was something they picked up 'through life'. However, whereas, more
fathers drew on the public sphere, mothers tended to draw on what they expected
from within the private sphere of the family, that is, what they picked up from the
outside was negatively valued in relation to what they thought their parents should
have been doing. If we return to Elizabeth Johnston:

> I didn't get any at school. I noticed that my mother had a little cutting
> from something that she was going to send away for, a book or something,
> but she never did. I was reading other girls' books at school that their
> mothers had given them.

Rather than direct her criticism at maternal neglect, in general, it was her own
mother who was seen as wanting. A similar point was made by Betty Deary, but
her criticism was directed at mothers in general.

> I know for a fact my mother never ever spoke tae me about anything. It
> was the most gruelling thing when you had tae listen tae other people. I
> think it's up tae the parents really to try and explain things like that. I went
> out into the wide world completely ignorant about these things . . . I always
> maintained our two kids would never go through life the way I did.

Again, allowing for the small numbers, we may be able to discern a pattern
here by drawing on notions of the public and private spheres as gendered categories.
Mothers were critical about what they felt their own mothers ought to have done.
A minority of fathers, however, were more ambivalent about their own past; simultaneously glorifying a rugged individualism of finding out for yourself in a world
outside the formal confines of the home, whilst stressing the importance of the
formal sources for their own children.[5]

What was surprising about discussions on sex education was the fact that
information on parents' own sex education was offered sometimes in an unsolicited fashion. Parents would invoke their own experiences as a means of comparison
with what their children were receiving or ought to be receiving. Parents would
contextualize the demands they made sometimes on themselves, but usually on the
schools, by referring to their own inadequate sex education. This inadequacy was
an important factor in shaping the ideas they had about how their own children
should be treated as future sexual beings.

This point can also be brought out if we refer to the limitations of these
accounts in using them to deduce anything about the parents' sexual lives. Sex
education was experienced by most of the parents as adolescents as a significant

social and moral lacuna. Yet there would appear to be little manifest evidence of this as a social problem for parents as sexual beings. Nothing was said about how their lack of sex education had affected their sex lives or their treatment of each other as sexual beings. Accounts of their pasts as children, rather than acting as indicators of their own 'inadequate socialization', were used as reference points as to how their own children ought to be treated.

Furthermore, the comparison between their own inadequate sex education and their children's 'need to know', was framed within a nascent sense of social change. Parents seemed to reflect some of the themes that run through the individualization thesis: the loss of moral and social certainties such as class, institution and locale (Büchner, 1990; Beck, 1992). Parents were arguing that there was a necessity now for their children to know about sex in a more informed manner. Parents were expressing the view that children were growing up in a more 'public' environment. Their world views were being shaped less by what was specific to their particular families and what was said by their own parents. This was exemplified by the Dobbies. Evelyn Dobbie talked in more general terms about the past experiences of parents.

> Depends on how you've been brought up yourself. A lot of people have been brought up where it's forgotten about. You end up getting no sex education and finding about it yourself. You end up growing up totally ignorant. I mean why have your kids totally ignorant to all these things going on. We dinnae just volunteer the information. You dinnae just come out and say it. If they ask questions you answer them as best as you can and make sure there's no embarrassment. We don't want them to be really shy about these things.

This was corroborated by her husband John who saw sex education as part of a much broader process of opening up the public arena to children.

> *JD*: My parents and Evelyn's parents were embarrassed. But we just bring it up in natural conversation.
>
> *MW*: What about the moral aspects?
>
> *JD*: AIDS and abortion are things that are talked about on the television, on the news and in the papers. Michael and Alison both read the newspaper and see the headlines. They're taught to do that in school though, which is something we were never encouraged to do.

The point being made here is that children are being encouraged now to discuss issues that were previously seen as only adult pursuits: the discussion of politics, morality and sexuality. Whereas the decline thesis might take this as just another indicator of the power of social and moral frames of reference outside of the family over the 'natural' authority of parents, the parents interviewed were more positive about the consequences for their children in terms of the high value placed on the commodity of knowledge. In Chapter 5 we saw how parents perceived their children as morally and socially naive – unprepared for the 'uncivil society'. Evidence from parental perception about their children's sexuality would appear to contradict this. In relation to sexual issues parents tended to see their children as being more mature; much more worldly about sex than they were at their age. George Terry brought out this point when comparing his own sex education with that of his three teenage sons: 'Sex was never mentioned when I was at school. They all know far more than I knew at their ages.' This adolescent worldliness was also a prominent feature in discussions with Will Barnes:

> I think you've got to give credit to the kids now. They are not that naive. They know what's going on socially. They are very aware, especially now. When he was younger he [his son] embarrassed us a couple of times because of the knowledge he had. You tended to think that at the age he was at the time he wouldn't have that knowledge. But I think that was because we were a bit backward in that respect. We didn't know that when we were younger.

AIDS and the Moral Limits of Schooling

In the previous chapter I suggested that the AIDS issue crystallized for teachers the problems of discussing sexual matters with children. For some, AIDS was a medium through which they were able to explore sensitive moral and social issues. For others, AIDS reinforced anxieties teachers had about sex education because it forced them to confront issues that might either be ignored (St Mary's and homosexuality) or immersed them within more general talk about 'relationships'.

If we turn to the parents, there was, in principle, no objection to AIDS being discussed within the classroom. Yet, anxiety was expressed by a few parents over the extent to which their children were privy to the details of how the virus might be contracted. A minority of parents here tended to conflate the role of the school with the role of the media in developing a public discourse on AIDS. There were two strands to this concern; the universal nature of the campaign, and the extent to which a moral dimension was being discussed. The Mctears both expressed the first anxiety.

> We are in an age now where children have got to know about these things. It's just how much they talk about it and how much they put it over. Some children are ready to accept, some children aren't, even although they are the same ages. I don't think they take these things into consideration . . . (Tom Mctear)

This view was corroborated by his wife.

I suppose they have to know. I cannae see Gordon, he's only thirteen. I know its happening; you lift a newspaper, you see it on television. I honestly think there's too much talk about sex . . . I don't really think Gordon's going to think about getting AIDS or Paula for that matter. My older son, I did say to him one night, 'Do you realize you have to take precautions these days?' (Anne Mctear)

There is the articulation again here of the ambivalence over the status of the adolescent. Both parents had very fixed views about how and when their children become autonomous sexual beings. The Mctears were representative of a minority of parents who didn't want their children exposed to the 'nitty gritty' of the homosexual act in the classroom.

Several other parents with religious convictions were more concerned about the moral stance the school was going to take and whether this conflicted with their own position. Again there was no objection to AIDS being discussed, but the advice that some of their children were given went against their own moral convictions. When asked whether he thought it was a good thing that AIDS and abortion were discussed in school, Will Barnes, a Catholic parent replied:

Yes, but it depends on what they are putting across. If it went against my beliefs I'd be against it in the school and I'd like to be made aware of it.

Kathleen Adams, a Baptist, was more specific about what she thought was unacceptable:

I saw one of the school's videos on AIDS. They said if you're going to have sex use a condom. I disagreed with them saying that. They should have encouraged them not to have sex in the first place. Schools should really push the no sex angle. But I do accept that there are stupid pupils where it's probably necessary to talk about condoms. For me, sex equals marriage.

Parents here echo the ambiguous concerns expressed through the Longford Report (Longford Committee, 1972). On the one hand, there is the fear that factual discussions encourage adolescents to experiment. On the other hand, there is a concern that the school doesn't go far enough in placing the sexual act within a traditional moral context.

These concerns need to be set against the more general feeling among the parents that the school was the most appropriate place to discuss AIDS. An extensive campaign conducted through the media was having a considerable impact on the schools' sex education curriculum. Television drew on the famous and the knowledgable through advertising and discussion in putting across explicit messages about how AIDS could be avoided. There was a general recognition throughout the schools that the AIDS situation warranted a considered and immediate reaction. Schools were able to present themselves as professionally competent teaching establishments to the parents. We have seen earlier in the chapter that this was only confirming what parents already thought about the school – that it was the most appropriate place for the dissemination of information on sex. Thus, rather than seeing the sex education in school as a symptom of a more general arena of public amorality, the school was seen as the safest place to discuss sex.

Most of the parents had received letters and leaflets from the school on what was going to be discussed. When discussing the immediacy of the problem Frank Rodgers stated that:

it needs to be touched on . . . I know in a lot of homes it's just not discussed. At least in school they get the facts and they get guidance.

This was echoed by John Dobbie. When asked whether the school should be discussing things likes AIDS and abortion, he answered:

Yes, it's a good thing. There might be some kids whose parents never bother to discuss these things. It'll definitely benefit them and won't do the others any harm. There might be things that we haven't covered. They might be able to help us in that matter. I cannae see it being harmful.

Sex Talk and the Parental Routine

In the previous section I was concerned with the more formal aspects of sex talk within the home, which tended to be seen by parents as problematic. Although many parents wanted to discuss sex with their children in a more formal manner, parents tended to see these encounters as dramatized moments which would create a great deal of embarrassment. Prendergast and Prout (1987, p. 82) made the point that children tend to rely on more routine sources for information about bringing up children and sex. Through direct experience of being around close family and other kin, and through more informal talk heard within the home and the local neighbourhood, children pick up more information about child rearing than they would from more formal discussions with either teachers or parents. This same approach might be applied to knowledge about sex.

In this section I outline situations described by parents where sex is discussed in an informal routine way with their children. Following this, I look at instances where parents try and contain discussions on sex within the family routine by normalizing situations where children confront parents with questions that are potentially embarrassing.[6]

Where parents had difficulty broaching the subject directly, sex was quite often discussed in relation to a third party. Parents might openly discuss a friend or relative who is having an affair or getting divorced. This was something that would sometimes crop up in daily discussion around the meal table. Parents' attitudes on extra-marital sex, divorce and teenage pregnancies will work their way through in these discussions. The Wilsons both expressed difficulties when discussing sex with their children. Both confessed that they were embarrassed and ill equipped to deal with their children's developing sexual awareness. Their daughter, Lynn, was 17 years old and had just met her first boyfriend. He was starting to spend more time in Lynn's room listening to records. Whereas her father tended to worry about the length of time they spent together on their own, her mother stated that she 'totally trusted them'. She spoke with confidence about this trust:

> The children know what you're talking about even within the family. George [her husband] has a brother who's had one wife then a girlfriend. His wife had a baby and this other girlfriend he's going about with now has got a baby. It's something we talk quite openly about. The kids'll discuss it and they'll say, 'What a way for Uncle Davy to carry on. He must have kids all over the place!' It's more that sort of thing . . . They obviously know they're sleeping together . . . you just come to an understanding that we know that they know the facts of life. They have quite strong views which they must have got from us at some stage. I'm quite happy that they've all got standards. (Jean Wilson)

Routine contacts with other adults outside of the home can also serve as opportunities for parents to discuss sexual behaviour and morality with children. This was brought out by Christine Terry who mentioned homosexual friends who regularly visited the house.

> I haven't said anything that I've shown prejudice about. A couple of chaps that regularly come round to see us are practising homosexuals. But I never say to the kids this is . . . he's a homosexual. It's like religion you hope that they sort things out for themselves and don't make any wrong decisions. I wouldn't say you mustn't.

Christine Terry took a fairly agnostic line when it came to morality. Her main worry was that the school would push any form of moral approach. She was particularly opposed to religious education.

> I've always assumed that these things had a balance in school. Someone had raised the point that the anti-abortion group had brought out a video that they were circulating in the schools and they weren't giving the other point of view. They did concede that you had to give a balanced view in sex education but to get round this they introduced it in religious education. I would certainly raise it with the school if they brought it in that way . . . A child has got to make up its own mind on certain things. I mean they could grow up absolutely anti-abortion and I'd be perfectly happy with that but they should have a balance so that they can decide these things for themselves.

For Christine Terry sex talk was more fully integrated in family life because she felt that to treat it as something out of the ordinary was to heighten a particular moral approach which would inhibit her sons' development of their moral autonomy. The fact that they had gay friends made it easier to talk about sexual morality within the home.

A more complex version of Christine Terry's approach was offered by Elisabeth Johnston. She saw sex education in terms of the fact/value distinction. The physiological aspects were easier to talk about:

> By the time John was eight he knew everything from amniocentesis (she had just given birth to Philip) to everything about childbirth. There was nothing biological he didn't know. It came as no surprise, there was nothing surprising for him.

Elizabeth had used her pregnancy – the birth of her second son – to discuss the physiology of sex with her eldest son. The birth of the second son was defined very much from within; very much a 'family matter'. Elizabeth was able to confidently draw on experiences that were defined uniquely in her own terms. At the same time she used her own experiences as an example of the general: what Elizabeth was going through was what all mothers were going through.

Although the physiology of sex was an integral part of the family routine, difficulties were encountered in talking about sex within a moral or ethical context. Unlike situations where parents would rather downplay more deliberate discussions about sex within the home, the moral and social aspects of sex were deliberately dramatized. When asked whether she had ever discussed the moral aspects she paused for a long time and said:

> I don't think we'd talk about that particularly . . . it has to, you know . . . obviously when we talk about marriages breaking up and responsibility for it or no responsibility for it . . . we've had a lot of friends whose marriages have split up. We've spoken about it, and John's watched the other children go through it . . . in a joking way, I think we've talked about how we got married or you know our relations before we got married . . . kidding in public in front of John about our different relations before, and John loves these stories.

The break up of many of Elizabeth's friends relationships were defined almost in terms of their inevitability. According to Elizabeth 'divorce is very common these days'. This created anxieties for Elizabeth because there was a question mark over how her children experience these breakups. Elizabeth's worry was how her own children perceived these breakdowns. There were two aspects to this: how John experiences his own friends' reactions to their parents breaking up, and more importantly here, how John interprets this in terms of his own parents' relationship.

These tensions made Elizabeth uneasy in trying to explain how sex works socially. Parents here cannot simply adopt the same intimate tones of the natural in talking about sex in terms of relationships. For parents there can be nothing routine about parental breakdown. This creates an obvious difficulty for parents in broaching the subject of their friends' breakups. Parents need to emphasize the exceptional nature of divorce in situations where divorce is happening to more of their friends.

In some instances these tensions can be offset by humour. The situation can at least be partially redeemed by drawing on stories about their sex lives before they were married. The curiosity of the child can be channelled through stories about the parents before they were married. When asked whether John ever talked about sex, Elizabeth replied:

> Yes, a little. I think sometimes he's testing us out here . . . but also . . . he's very forward with telling us his new jokes. I think it's also his way of asking us what this means or telling us 'look what I know now!'

Jokes were his way of introducing the subject of sex into conversation. This clearly, corresponds to his parents' tentative approach to the problem of sex as a moral subject for discussion.

Humour featured in other households as a response to public awareness of the AIDS issue. Families were subject to detailed information on the homosexual and heterosexual act, emphasis being placed on the use of contraceptives as a necessary precursor to sexual intercourse. A few of the parents mentioned the influence of the campaign through the almost institutionalized usage of the word 'condom'. Their children were starting to use the word in conversation with other members of the family. Alice White laughed at how easily this had been accepted within the family.

> They get a lot from the television. Ian is at the awkward age, he's sniggery aboot it the now. But Jim seems tae be taking it in. His dad and my brother, the things that they are saying to them, to Jim the now, they're slagging him about condoms and all the rest o' it. The jokes that are passed between them sort o' makes it easier for them now. Then Jim will come hame wie' a new joke for his dad and he'll say, 'dinnae you let your mother hear that!'

Jim's father was able to offset some of the tension felt when the subject of sex arose because he was able to joke with his son about a 'serious' socio–moral matter. When going out to the school dance he would joke with his son by reminding him 'no' tae forget his condoms'.

Television and the Normalization of Sex

The television was another medium through which sex was discussed in the home. This is reflected in recurrent public debates over the power and influence of the media. Questions of taste, choice and censorship have been expressed which high-light the distinctions made between 'external' and 'internal' censorship of what children watch on television. Should there be state censorship or should parents be left to determine what their children watch?[7] In my sample, parents oscillated between these two positions. Sex on television can embarrass both parents and children. For the parents, part of the problem is feeling that they have a duty to respond to what they see as unsuitable or risky programmes. Some parents will actively censor what their children watch by anticipating programmes that are thought to be too sexually explicit. Others will invoke their own version of the nine o'clock threshold as a way of screening out potentially unacceptable programmes. Jim Short outlines his views on this:

> I'm an old-fashioned father and I don't like it [sex] being mentioned. I don't watch much television but if I see something risky coming on I tend to chase them.

The television, though, can be used more positively by parents in trying to normalize sex within the home. Parents deliberately avoided heightening sex as something special and treated it like any other subject that comes up in conversation. For George Terry this was case of:

> . . . trying not to make anything out to be a big deal. You can have very explicit programmes on television and they just watch and sometimes they ask what's going on and we tell them.

Ian Davies recounted how he coped when his 11-year-old son asked him what rape was after having picked up the word from the television.

> I said something like, it's a very serious assault on a woman by a man. I thought at that stage that would be enough. I tend to give the answer that would suffice under the circumstances. But I also think you need to answer their questions as casually as possible. That is, not to sound too . . . heighten it. Make it as casual and normal as possible.

For Frank Rodgers the unexpected sex scene on television and the aspects of the sexual vocabulary questioned by their children, although still embarrassing, are occasions for discussion and clarification. When I asked him if sex ever cropped up in normal discussion, he said:

> Oh yes, last night for instance. They mentioned the word 'impotent' on television. They asked what was that? We told them. It just came up in natural conversation.

Conclusion

In Chapters 5 and 6 I have laid out the problem of sex education as viewed from parental and teaching perspectives. In the concluding passages I want to compare these perspectives indicating, initially, points of convergence. First, both parents and teachers stressed the importance of sex education by drawing on a changing social and moral environment. In particular, reference is made to the way that the AIDS crisis crystallizes these changes in that it balances issues of moral, social and physical risk against the older certainties of development, 'timing' and positional differences. Social change here is identified by both parents and teachers as the opening up of the public sphere to children. This has the contradictory effect of strengthening the child's 'right to know' and increasing the demands made on adults to regulate the effects of this which in turn reinforces an adult's 'right to know'.

A second and associated area where parents and teachers meet, at least those that have strong religious convictions, is over the attempt to impose limits on the AIDS knowledge that their children or pupils have access to. The relative success of these forms of censorship throws up an interesting question: whether the home or the school is the most effective censor. In relation to sex education a provisional answer favours the school, with St Mary's being able to construct more tangible limits on what sex education consists of in school through a form of collective omission. Yet, I have already referred to the problems that parents and teachers have regulating their children's social and moral development within a relatively unconstrained public environment. The question may therefore be less pertinent, for the issue is one of regulating rather than limiting the child's exposure to 'adult' ideas.

A third, more straight-forwardly consensual area is the position of mothers in sex education. Whether we are talking about actual, normative or 'lay theoretical' understandings of a division of labour within the home, mothers are seen as the responsible agents. We have to rely on more phenomenological accounts about the family routine to assess the roles that fathers play.

A final point where teaching and parental perspectives intersect is over the difficulties experienced teaching and discussing sex education. The discomfort felt by both parents and teachers appears to transcend the very different contexts within which sex education takes place. Although this similarity of experience is complicated by the gendered nature of sex education in both the home and the classroom, parents and teachers had problems bringing sex talk within their respective paradigms of adult authority. One of the ironies of sex education here is that, as I have already outlined, problems that parents and teachers have are experienced within a context of more public talk about sex. The Foucaultian notion of a discourse on sex is pertinent here (Foucault, 1976). The importance of AIDS, the problem of child sex abuse and the concerns over censorship and teenage pregnancies are articulated through a framework of prohibition and control. Those who have legitimate moral and social responsibilities for young people are put under more pressure. Although there is an underlying sense that sex education ought to be undertaken informally by parents, teachers, oddly enough, appear to have a keener sense of responsibility. The recent pragmatic shift towards schooling as the focus for sex education, the increase in importance attached to sex education and the confidence that parents had in the school's ability to deliver sex education, a confidence picked up by the teachers themselves, seems to have sharpened the teachers' awareness of their positions as sex educators.

Nevertheless, although we might argue here that an expanding discourse on sex constrains those with responsibilities for sex education, there is also a sense in which the discourse opens up the possibilities and pretexts for sex education. Sexual images and language through the media and an adult sexual lexicon freely drawn on by children were used by teachers and parents consciously and semi-consciously as vehicles through which more pedagogic attempts were made at discussing the physiology and morality of sex. They were also, importantly, occasions for monitoring what the child already knew.

One final point concerns a clearly discernible tension between the parental and teaching definitions of who ought to have responsibility for sex education. In one obvious sense this is the shifting – we might even say the delegating – of an unwanted adult responsibility on to the significant adult other. But there is little symmetry here. Teachers differentiated between a *de jure* responsibility, parental primacy, and a pragmatic and professional commitment to the child's welfare. From the parents' point of view a desire to take control over the child's sexual development cannot easily be squared with the confidence expressed by parents over sex education in school. Yet, clearly for some parents this inconsistency is less marked where the technical know-how of the guidance teacher appears to override any strong inner sense of responsibility.

Another way of expressing this inconsistency is to balance the parents' need to know how their children develop sexually, and the contention that their adolescent children have a right to be fully informed about the moral 'risks and opportunities' confronting them. As in Chapter 4, the tension between parents' 'rights' and the adolescent's desire for independence are much less harshly felt if we can identify more routine and less interventionist means by which parents are able to monitor their children's sexuality. By drawing on the more routine levels of parenting, I identified the informal modes of communication that parents used to keep abreast of their children's developing sexualities. We might also add that parents are in a much stronger position at this informal level to check that their children were picking up the 'right' values.

Notes

1   Social class does not loom large in the most recent and comprehensive study of sex education, Isobel Allen's *Education in Sex and Personal Relationships*, 1987. Where it is discussed is in relation to parental advocacy of the school. Slightly more working-class parents than middle-class parents favoured the school introducing the topic (Allen, 1987, p. 87).

2   The figure was 60 per cent in the Allen study (Allen, 1987, p. 87).

3   See Appendix 2.

4   There is an interesting discussion about the limitations of relying solely on 'first recollections of "learning" about reproduction' in Farrell (1978, pp. 54–5).

5   In the Allen study, 63 per cent of mothers were dissatisfied with their own sex education, whereas only 41 per cent of the fathers expressed the same opinion. This would appear to correspond with the gender difference (1987, p. 107).

6   Giddens offers an interesting distinction between life events which disrupt the routine,

such as births and deaths, and critical situations which are almost exclusively contingent. Whereas the former can still be conceptualized as part of the routine in that life events are not necessarily unpredictable, the latter are situations that social actors face which are so unpredictable that they lead to social disorientation. Sexual pedagogy is an interesting case in that although parents are continually predicting when they will bring up the subject of sex (the procrastination), there is also a sense of social disorientation in the singular nature of the interaction (Giddens, 1984, pp. 60–1).

7 References to this debate ran through *The Times* editorial columns in the mid-1980s. For some examples, see: 28.11.85; 21.2.86; 22.10.86. More recently, in the aftermath of the Jamie Bulger case, censorship and parenting has become a public issue again. See P. Wintour 'Bulger judge urges debate on parent and videos', *The Guardian*, 27.1.93, p. 1; E. Gorman 'Horror videos do not turn children into horrific people', *The Times*, 26.11.93, p. 3; A. Leathley 'Howard hints at censorship laws on video violence', *The Times*, 22.1.94, p. 8.

Public Policy and the 'Responsible Parent'

In this book I have tried to capture, in some phenomenological sense, the bound-aries of parents' responsibilities and account for the social and moral roles of those outside of the home who have 'claims' on their children. Over the last fifteen years, politicians, commentators and social scientists have drawn, redrawn and refined this boundary in the light of an alleged assault on the integrity of the family by the state. Yet, as the Newsons argue, the nature of what parents are supposed to do within these boundaries remains elusive.

> Parents are in fact chronically on the defensive over their parental role because the responsibility laid on them is not only limitless but supremely personal. (Quoted in Harris, 1983, p. 240)

The 'personalized and limitless' nature of parental responsibility is partly a product of the intermingling of biology, culture and political pressure. But there is also an important temporal commitment that generates a contradiction within the practice of parenthood. The concept of primacy signifies the parent as the first and most important influence – a reminder to the outside world that parents still carry the major responsibilities. This gives parents a sense of propriety and ownership. Despite some parental equivocation, it also means that parents have to accept the consequences of the different ways that their children present themselves to the outside world. Yet, although it appears that being first on the scene and 'knowing your child' gives a parent certain rights, there is ultimately a sense in which parenting has a purpose beyond sustaining a child's physical and social well-being, a function which leads to the negation of their status.

In an individualistic culture, primacy also means that parents are normatively responsible for producing the 'responsible' individual. We can see the process of parents directing their children towards an independent status as the 'withering away' of parental authority. Parents, then, not only have to contend with the seem-ingly endless accretion of tasks across time, they have to know when is the appro-priate time to restrict these tasks in the interests of the children's development.

These dilemmas for parents can be further illustrated if we return to the notion of responsibility for disciplining children. Both parents and teachers, in their accounts, constantly return to the theme of 'bringing up' children. Like the notion of prim-acy this can be taken as a boundary-setting device that separates parents from other authority figures outside of the home. But it also refers to the all-encompassing nature of living with children and dealing with their problems on a routine basis. Bringing up children for some parents signifies a degree of latitude in interpreting their responsibilities. This can mean a degree of give and take in relation to boundary setting within the home. There is an interesting comparison here between discipline and authority exercised within the home and the classroom. The more circumscribed range of teaching functions and the institutional backing for school discipline according to some parents appear to make it easier for teachers to discipline their children. Without a hint of resentment, George Terry seemed to sum up this feeling among the parents.

> I hope it's very noticeable with my three [sons] that if a teacher says something to them they believe it, they trust it and do it. They feel obliged . . . they tend to listen to teachers much more than they listen to parents. I've no doubt other parents would say the same thing.

As I have argued, the present discourse on state intervention sets up negative images of those outside of the home who have claims on the child's well-being. But we learn very little about the routinized 'irrationalities' associated with parenting. From a parental perspective those agencies, like the school, that are doing the same kinds of things as parents yet have legitimate claims over the child's welfare are bound to be more successful than the parents themselves. This is reflected at the macro level with the educational debate focusing on the simple traditionalism that ought to be brought back into classroom discipline (Alexander, Rose and Whitehead, 1992). This is not to say that classroom control is in practice easier to achieve: Chapter 2 demonstrates the different ways in which an uneasy mix of educational and moral elements are maintained by teachers in keeping the upper hand in class. Furthermore, these skills are acknowledged by some parents. What is being presented by parents here is some notion that the ill-defined and ever expanding nature of parental discipline compares less favourably with the rule bound nature of teaching where there is some degree of external assessment of 'good' and 'bad' discipline in class and where there is a professional separation between teacher and pupil. Parents, quite simply, lack the guidelines that they imagine inform the teaching role.

Moral Uncertainty and Shared Responsibilities

Although parents sustained a proprietorial sense of themselves as moral guardians, the simple lack of fixed guidelines can lead to parents drawing on external support from the school in maintaining both the integrity of their children's moral and physical well-being and their own sense of self. We might see this as an inconsistency in their accounts of themselves as parents, but there is no simple abdication of responsibility here. We might again refer to the routine business of parenting. The development of a sophisticated monitoring system, the active renegotiation of public and private spheres, and the normalizing and semi-conscious surveying of the child's sexual development, were all ways that parents underwrote their children's welfare.

The techniques of control were, in part, responses to the ill-defined nature of bringing up children. I have argued that discipline and control are cultural attributes of parenting in that the parents and teachers interviewed saw them as central features of their responsibilities. Despite the particular approach that a parent might profess to subscribe to, all parents were in the business of boundary setting and sanctioning as part of the daily flow of parental activities, what Giddens (1984, p. 3) calls the *durée* of social life. But, parents' disciplinary activities were also responses to general perceptions of the outside world as a realm of moral and social uncertainty. This uncertainty has been interpreted more positively by social theorists in terms of notions of risk and opportunity (Giddens, 1991; Beck, 1992). Yet, parents to some extent here have always grappled with these issues in that the general push away from the home into the outside world involves parents coming to terms both with the temptations open to their adolescent children and with the conjectures they make about how they respond to them. In Chapter 6, parents expressed posit-ive notions about their children's ability to negotiate the risks and opportunities surrounding their sexual development. But, in the main, these ideas were over-shadowed by the fears that they had about an uncivil society.

In constructing images of an uncivil society, parents, first of all, referred to their own adolescent experiences. Interestingly, parents were not offering a simple and consistent picture of a golden past. In part, this was due to the gendered nature of these experiences with fathers having more of a tendency to glorify the public sphere as a realm of sexual adventure and conquest. More generally, parents tended to highlight the importance of their children's sex education in the home and the school by referring to the inadequate level of sex education offered by their own parents and teachers when they were children. Yet, parents offered more positive images of their past when discussing their leisure time. The restricted space and 'protected liberation' offered their children now was compared less favourably with their own adolescent freedom in relation to public spaces.

More importantly, the notion of moral and physical vulnerability corresponds to general fears voiced about the ability of the young to develop a healthy and responsible social identity. The sexual and public realms, in one sense, are two sides of the same coin: opposing but complementary elements that make up the adult social identity. Notions of supervision and control of these realms always structure the parents' sense of self and underpin, in very routine ways, the responsibilities they have towards their children. Yet, parents also expressed a sophisticated under-standing of their adolescent children's needs which made these responsibilities more precarious and, ultimately, more negotiable. As I have argued, this didn't take the form of overt exchanges around the positional differences between parents and children. But parents acknowledged their adolescent children's changing status in the ways that they adopted strategies for keeping tabs on them.

Parents may, as Seabrook (1982) argues, be projecting their own inadequacies onto the outside world in the way they construct images about the uncivil society. Parents may, in fact, be susceptible to the impact of messages about AIDS and the dual concern of the child as victim and offender. But to present parents as powerless and alienated is to obscure the ways that they adapt to these circumstances and cope with their fears.

The Parentocracy

Given the all-encompassing nature of parenthood it would be difficult to conceive of parents offering one consistent image of themselves in relation to the outside world. The phenomenology of parenting focuses on the negotiation of roles and expectations in relation to the more intangible aspects of social life. The contingencies inherent in parental practice here mean that parents take a more pragmatic view of their roles. Parents try to sustain a predominant image of themselves as sovereign authority figures. But from time to time, circumstances dictate that parents become more reliant on the school's tutelage. There is an element of rationality here with parents appearing to delegate responsibility to the school. But there is also a sense that 'working at being a parent' means accepting what is available in a more routine unreflexive sense (Morgan, 1985, p. 186).

Nevertheless, we still need to make sense of the conflicting self-images that parents present. The idea that the parent is both separate from and dependent on the school has interesting parallels with the conflicting ways that the concept of the *responsible parent* is invoked in current educational and political thinking. In the final passages I will relate these images with current sets of dominant ideas and values which impinge on parental and teaching practice.

As I outlined in the first chapter, critics of the interventionist state set up a radically different vision of society. The welfare state is to be replaced by some form of civil society based on Adam Smith's 'invisible hand' with the family as the basic unit of society (Adam Smith Institute, 1985). Parents become the sole focal point for the moralizing and socializing of children. The school, like other external agencies of social support, is contracted in, bought in, even, at an early stage to educate their children.

The 1988 Education Reform Act is a key legislative attempt at restructuring relations between 'individuals' and the state by shifting the balance of power between parents and teachers. A weak version of this is suggested by the 'parents' charter' which has been added to the political lexicon as political parties debate the relative merits of a contractual relationship between parent and teacher.[1] More fundamentally, this vision of society is bound up with the notion of the parentocracy with the parent in a new role as 'citizen consumer' (Woods, 1988; Meighan, 1989; Brown, 1990). Two key modes of parent–teacher relations are suggested here: the parent as controller of the education process and the parent as consumer.

Parent as Controller

The idea that parents have more control over the education process is linked to the local management of schools (LMS), and in Scotland the introduction of school boards, both central planks of recent educational reform. Although subject to central government approval, the 1988 act allows parents to vote on schools opting out of local government control. The financial, organizational and day-to-day running subsequently become the responsibility of a small governing body with parents of children from that school becoming majority 'shareholders'.

In previous chapters I suggested that parents and teachers, in the abstract, had a strong sense of the respective spheres of influence of the home and the school. Within this framework the formal educational requirements of the child were best left to the professional expertise of the teachers. Although the evidence is far from conclusive, discussions with parents around the more specific aspects of the 'parentocracy' tended to reinforce this position.[2] The majority of parents displayed little enthusiasm for their new found powers in policing the schools. Twenty-two (50 per cent) parents were opposed to any significant change in the way the schools were run. Whereas twelve parents (27 per cent) wanted more consultation and closer parent–teacher links. But this stopped well short of what we might term 'parent power'. The great majority of parents did not think that they had any right to dictate to teachers how the school should be run. There was a spectrum of opinion which flowed from a reticence to get involved – they had neither the time nor the inclination – to a complete rejection of the principle of parental intrusion into the school. The following quotes from a working-class and middle-class parent illustrate this point.

> I know nothing whatsoever about teaching and I feel, you know, I couldn't sit on a board and dictate to teachers that you should be doing this, that and the next thing. (Ruby Bolton)

> I don't think that parents are qualified. They don't know what they're expected to do. I don't think that I'm qualified. I'm no' saying that parents shouldn't have a say, but they should be guided by the teachers . . . Are they going to be able to change teachers? That's absolute rubbish. How could I decide who is a good teacher. I'd have to be a teacher to know. (George Wilson)

Parent as Consumer

The idea of the parent as consumer would appear, on the face of it, to have more appeal because it corresponds to the concept of primacy as a set of rights that parents have over other socializing agencies. Primacy, in a very general sense, is all about knowing your child best and knowing what is best for your child. Within a free market ideology, this can be translated into a form of monetary shorthand through the concept of consumer sovereignty. Parents know better than the state what their child needs educationally. The market offers a choice; educational vouchers become a virtual reality as parents exercise their bargaining powers with schools being compelled to display their wares in the form of league tables on exam results (educational achievement) and truancy rates (educational failure).

Within this ideological framework, the content of education – the National

Curriculum – no longer remains in conflict with parental choice. Parents are assumed to make the connections between 'national standards' and educational outcomes. With regular testing of their children in class, parents have a running commentary on their children's achievements and, more importantly, a means by which their children's achievements can be measured against the school's averages and the school's achievements can be measured against other schools.

From the data, empirical validation of this is difficult.[3] This version of the educational market place has only recently been completed – the publication of league tables on educational performance coming too late to be discussed by the parents in this study. Nevertheless, parents were asked about the concept of choice by referring to the Parents' Charter of 1981 (Education Act [Scotland]) which allowed parents to send their children to schools outside of their catchment area. Parents at this stage were relatively less informed when making choices, relying on local knowledge rather than more objective assessments of the schools' performances. Again, the evidence is limited.

Parents were asked about decisions regarding the 'choice' of their children's secondary schools. Most parents when prompted were aware of the long waiting lists for magnet schools in other parts of the city. A few parents indicated that an informed choice had been made with the child's happiness and the close proximity of the local secondary school having more force than the more abstract and uncertain attractions of a desired magnet school. But the vast majority of these parents claimed that they had not 'chosen' their children's secondary school in any meaningful sense.[4] Thus, although parents were aware of the possibilities of sending their children to any school within the region, a considerable number tended to deny that the concept of parental choice existed.

One possible answer was that parents were aware of the theoretical possibility of sending their child to a school with a good reputation, but the kinds of schools they had in mind – usually the same three 'best' schools in the region – were so difficult to get into that the very process of weighing up the pros and the cons was a non-starter. Following on from this, it maybe that these parents still tended to refer to an older culture of choice by invoking the independent/state school system divide. For these parents choice was irrelevant because 'choosing' schools only made any sense where a parent was in the financial position to be able send their child to a private school. Choosing a school – and the free market for education – was still restricted to the private sector.

The sample size precludes any inferential leap about the general receptiveness of the new parental role, but parents in this study were clearly less than enamoured with their roles as controllers of education. The notion of the parent as consumer, strictly speaking, does not work at the economic level for there is little sense in which parents actually consume education (Deem, 1990, p. 161). It works more at a political and psychological level because it appeals to the parent as the mythical rational individual conquering the evils of the collectivist state. The notion of the responsible parent here suggests that the new market order deprives the state of its power by mythically returning all responsibilities for child development back to parents and thus reinforcing the idea of parental primacy.

Public Order, Schooling and Welfare

I have argued that the general fears parents had of children being 'out of place', foreshadowed the role the school was expected to play in supervising their children's moral and physical well-being. This feeds directly into a public order agenda with the focus on the public accountability of parents in preventing truancy and juvenile crime. The 'responsible parent', therefore, not only figures in the discourse on educational reform, it plays a prominent role on the public order agenda.

The ideology of individualism only works on the basis of a psychological appeal to the parents' sense of self as a sovereign authority figure. Within this model parent–child relations are inferred from relations between parent and outside agency. Parents recapture their rights: little is said about what parents do with them. Given the current agenda of child protection and questions about the supervision of children's time away from the home, the focus of attention is the quality of relations between parent and child. The appeal to privacy and individualism as a set of rights, then, is countered here through the expression of these rights as public *obligations*.

The 1991 public disturbances in Oxford and Tyneside and the more recent concerns expressed about juvenile crime have generated a lengthy public assessment of the causes of public disorder (Dean, 1993; Utting, 1993). This commentary, to some extent, reflects lay social theories offered by the guidance teachers in Chapter 3 – loss of parental authority, a general breakdown in communication compounded by impoverished economic circumstances. Furthermore, the blaming of parents would appear to be reinforced as 'solutions' suggested by a recent Home Office White Paper (1992) focus on penalizing parents of children in trouble.

But public analysis is ambiguous here. Responsibility for public order is held to be a more collective enterprise as teachers as well as parents are held responsible for public disorder.[5] In one sense 'responsibility' here is secondary in that commentators question the ability of the school to contain the problem. The notion that children are now out of control in school reflects the breakdown in division of responsibility between home and school suggested by teachers in Chapter 3 – teachers are unable to exert control in class because parents are not providing them with 'school trained' children. But there is a stronger sense in which the responsibility teachers have for public disorder is on a par with parents. The analyses of disorder in class, focus on educational causes such as a loss of educational authority and the adoption of child-centred teaching practices. Educational 'solutions' have been provided by others in the form of teaching citizenship in primary schools.[6] What is in effect being argued here is that notions of child-centredness and loss of authority are indicators of a more general moral decline where parents and teachers are culpable because they represent the loss of adult authority (Daley, 1991). This, interestingly, seems to converge with assessments made by the working-class parents interviewed in this study.

The differences between the educational and public order discourses can be seen as a tension between the invocation of the responsible parent in individualized and collectivized forms; the tension between responsibilities as right and responsibilities as obligations. But the problem is not simply the selective use of the 'responsible parent' in the promotion of disparate and unpopular public policies.[7] The tension is one of education as part of the free market order undermining attempts at dealing with the rising incidence of youthful indiscipline and disorder. The most recent Education Act (1993) brings the two discourses together by making head teachers more accountable for problems caused by children 'out of place'. First, the school can no longer permanently exclude problem pupils. Second, the head teacher has the option of making arrangements for problem pupils to go into 'pupil referral centres'. This is, interesting, not so much because it can be taken as confirmation that juvenile crime is a public responsibility, but because these new measures need to be seen as a way of dampening down the implications of the 1988 Education Reform Act for public order. These implications have been spelt out in some detail elsewhere (Carlen *et al.*, 1992; Pyke, 1992). Given the welfare role of the schools in this study they are summarized briefly here.

First, the effects of the market place coupled with the weakening of local authority responsibilities for enrolment potentially increase the numbers of problem children excluded from school; children permanently out of place, children referred to within the public order agenda as both victims and offenders of juvenile crime (Pyke, 1992). As exclusion rates rise, schools like Boreston Community school and Stenhouse Academy, that had a reputation for accommodating pupils discarded by other schools, become overloaded.

Second, overloading may prove to be an optimistic scenario. Boreston and Stenhouse would not be well placed in the league tables which equate 'good' schools solely in terms of exam scores. Although local political pressures may limit the consequences of the reform act, schools that have an expertise in dealing with difficult pupils may simply disappear all together as parents move their children to schools much higher up the league tables.

What schools like Stenhouse offer, according to the teachers, was a network of intangible moral and social support for problem children and troubled parents hidden in the expected parental rush for places at quantifiably 'better' schools.

Third, I mentioned earlier the effects of testing and the National Curriculum on the time and energy needed by teachers to devote to non-curricular activities. Although there have been recent official moves towards centring personal and social education in schools – not least the Dearing attempt to free up 20 per cent of the teacher's curricular time – the non-curricular activities such as sex education are still vulnerable in a climate where school timetables are dominated by subjects that can be translated into a monetary shorthand of exam results.[8] This is particularly the case for schools with a general ethos and approach that goes beyond the traditional maxims of pedagogy and firm discipline. Schools like Boreston and Stenhouse, which prided themselves on their Catholicity of teaching approaches and their links with the local community, will have fewer options open to them in acting in the best interests of the child and the local community (Chitty, 1989, p. 178).

More generally, I have documented the way guidance feeds into discipline and provides a network of support for children and their parents. I would argue that moral and social support from the school on which parents rely for shaping their children's social identities is threatened by free market and pedagogic imperatives that dominate current education thinking. It may be that I am overstating the case here. As was argued earlier, the realm of policies and values shapes but does not foreclose the possibilities of action. Nevertheless, concerns that parents have over their children's well-being are hardly likely to be assuaged by an education system that no longer acts as a social and moral guarantor.

Notes

1 The parents' charter was an important feature of the electoral manifestos of the major political parties in early 1992. Labour produced a social contract version in an attempt to shift the agenda away from the individualism implicit in the Government's charter. See *Times Education Supplement*, 7.2.92, p. 9.

2 Although the idea of parent power was quite new at the time of the interviews, parents were being canvassed for their votes for the setting up of the school boards and were being sent information about their new powers as school governors. On the basis of this it seemed appropriate to question parents on these new 'powers'.

3 See David (1993, ch. 7) for a discussion of the theoretical and methodological considerations of work done on parental choice.

4 Ball, Bowe and Gewitz (1995) suggest that things have moved on since then in terms of different social class contexts of choice.

5 The Government 'Back to Basics' campaign and attempts by the Labour Party to shape the public order agenda have generated recent interest around the disciplinary role of the school. See 'Patten spells out code to tighten school discipline', *The Times*, 14.2.94; 'Blair pledges high standards and firm discipline in schools', *The Times*, 27.7.94.

6 See 'Borstals: primary schools in citizenship', *Independent on Sunday*, 28.2.93.

7 Much has been made of this contradiction in 'New Right' terms between the individualistic and traditionalist strands of thought (Levitas, 1986). Thatcherism could be seen as a successful attempt at integrating populist versions of both of these ideological positions. See Hall (1983).

8 Interestingly, the Citizenship Foundation recently advocated placing citizenship within the curricular mainstream, thus rendering it 'testable'. *Times Education Supplement* 5.3.93, p. 10.

Appendix 1

Teaching Sample

I interviewed twenty teachers from five Scottish secondary schools located within and around a medium-sized commercial city. I decided to look at guidance teachers from the general teaching population for three reasons. First, guidance staff had an important pastoral role to play in underwriting the social and emotional aspects of the child's education. Guidance thus dealt with the child's 'welfare' in the much broader 'holistic' sense. Secondly, guidance staff occupied a mediate position between the school and the home, and were presumed to have a more informed opinion of parents. Where parents have problems they wanted to discuss with the school, they tend to be the first point of contact. Where the school needed to approach parents, the guidance staff were usually relied upon to make the initial contact. Thirdly, guidance teachers divided up their time between their pastoral responsibilities and their classroom teaching.

Although the sample may not be strictly representative of the wider teaching community, their 'teaching' credentials were preconditions of their promotion to the guidance post. As well as having pastoral responsibilities, their own subject teaching was something in which they were still very much involved. Only three teachers commented on how their guidance work had significantly reduced their teaching timetable, and one of those had managerial responsibilities. The point being made here is that their pastoral responsibilities gave them unique insights into the backgrounds of the children. Within the context of the research interview this did not always prejudice the ways they were able to make sense of the children's backgrounds as more conventional classroom pedagogues and disciplinarians.

Four guidance teachers were interviewed from each of the five schools. In two of the smaller schools this was a process of self-selection – these schools having only four guidance teachers. The teachers in the other schools were chosen mainly on the basis of availability. The following table shows the major characteristics:

1   *St Mary's Roman Catholic School*
Reputation: good academically, tough on discipline

Name	Age	Subject	Experience
Bill Short **	56	Religious educ/AHT	28 (17)
Ian Jones	40	Maths	10 (1)
Ian Dury	52	Modern languages	23 (17)
Mary James **	43	Remedial	16 (12)

* Figures in brackets relate to guidance experience in years
** these teachers had children of their own

2   *Waterston High School*
Reputation: 'magnet' school

Name	Age	Subject	Experience
Ian Howe **	44	Technical	16 (15)
Bill Smart **	33	Physical education	10 (6)
Vivien Willis	45	Maths	24 (18)
Liz Sim **	63	English	13 (8)

3   *Stenhouse Academy*
Reputation: 'sink' school with child-centred approach

Name	Age	Subject	Experience
Jean Bryce **	63	Remedial/English	18 (8)
Norah Bowles **	31	Biology	5 (1)
Ruth Smith	41	Home economics	19 (16)
Ian Hart **	49	Chemistry	3 (.25)

4   *Boreston Community School*
Reputation: progressive, community-centred

Name	Age	Subject	Experience
Jim Craig **	39	Technical	10 (5)
Susan Bruce	34	English	11 (.25)
Joan Leslie	42	English/history	20 (16)
Alice Tay **	39	Biology	14 (9)

5   *Logan High School*
Reputation: 'low morale', 'sink' school

Name	Age	Subject	Experience
Dorothy Small	52	English	28 (18)
George Barry **	56	Technical	26 (17)
Anne Smart	37	History	15 (8)
Stewart Ross	40	Physical education	18 (9)

From the above we can see that a potential ambiguity lay between 'teaching' and 'parenting' for eleven of the teachers. Several means were used to ensure that they were always being addressed as 'professionals'. As I was interested in the assumptions, lay theories and understandings that teachers had of their pastoral responsibilities, the interviews were informal and semi-structured. There was thus less of an emphasis placed on standardizing the questions. Wherever possible, the teachers were unambiguously addressed as teachers. A few of the questions could be answered as parent or teacher (the teachers were aware that a sample of parents were being interviewed as part of the wider study). Teachers often helped to clarify this by prefacing their answers with, 'Are you asking me as a teacher or parent?' Finally, the teachers were all interviewed in school. The intention here was that the interview setting would reinforce the idea that teachers were being asked to comment on their professional lives.

Parental Sample

Middle-Class Parents

Iris Alison, 42, hairdresser, self-employed, PTA at primary school (1)
Bob Alison, 46, Garage/ welding business
Religion: Catholic
Married: 17 years
Children: Peter 15, Colin 11, Ian 8

Rita Barnes, 44, care assistant in a nursing home (1)
Will Barnes, 44, Area manager of sales company
Religion: Catholic
Married: 19 years
Children: William 15

Mary Bone, 37, housewife (2)
Ronald Bone, 42, Computer manager,
Religion: Protestant
Married: 15 years
Children: Kathleen 14, Susan 11

Alice Davies, 43, housewife (2)
Ian Davies, 43, Computer adviser for NHS
Religion: Baptist
Married: 17 years
Children: Alison 14, Anthony 11, Billy 8

Evelyn Dobbie, 36, primary school auxiliary (part-time) (1)
John Dobbie, 39, Garage owner
Religion: Catholic
Married: 15 years
Children: Michael 14, Alison 11, Anne 7

Elizabeth Johnston, 42, university researcher, (part-time)★★
Arthur Johnston, 46, public relations officer with the NHS
Religion: Jewish

Married: 15 years
Children: John 14, Bruce 3

Anne McTear, 42, NHS Staff Nurse (part-time) (3)
Tom McTear, 44, Police Constable
Religion: Protestant
Married: 19 years
Children: Paula 15, Gordon 13, William 18

Alice Rodgers, 36, housewife (4)
Frank Rodgers, 39, social worker, chairman of school council
Religion: Baptist
Married: 16 years
Children: Ronald 15, Jeff 12, John 11, Ruth 8

Jan Short, 41, housewife (2)
Jim Short, 44, sub fire officer and self-employed builder
Religion: Protestant
Married: 20 years
Children: Angela 15, Elizabeth 12

Agnes Slaney, 41, housewife (3)
Brian Slaney, 42, company director of construction business
Religion: Protestant
Married: 19 years
Children: June 17, Alan 14

Christine Terry, 57, shop assistant (part-time) (4)★
George Terry, 58, civil servant
Religion: atheist
Married: 29 years
Children: Tim 14, Stephen and Richard 12

Jean Wilson, 47, hotel proprietor (4)
George Wilson, 47, hotel proprietor
Religion: Protestant
Married: 25 years
Children: Lynn 17, Philip 15, Donald 13

Working-Class Parents

Kathleen Adams, 40, NHS clerk (part-time) (1)
George Adams, 44, clerk with British Telecom
Religion: Scottish Episcopalian

Married: 16 years
Children: Sally 14, Jim 10

Ruby Bolton, 42, housewife (1)
Bill Bolton, 44, clerk in an engineering business
Religion: Protestant
Married: 16 years
Children: Mary 14, Andrew 13

Betty Deary, 41, home help (part-time) (3)
Dave Deary, 51, sheet metal worker
Religion: Protestant
Married: 16 years
Children: Billy 15, Jean 13

Isabel Hart, 39, cleaner (part-time) (3)
Tom Hart, 40, slater
Religion: Protestant
Married: 19 years
Children: Thomas 15, Doreen 18

Rena Mckay, 53, housewife, ex. PTA (1)
Bill Mckay, 57, coach builder
Religion: Catholic
Married: 28 years
Children: Gillian 14 (Michael 26, Jane 25, Grant 24)

Jean Robbie, 42, NHS nursing auxiliary (1)
Ian Robbie, 44, NHS hospital porter
Religion: Catholic
Married: 15 years
Children: Donald 15, Alexander 17

Alice Roper, 35, housewife ★★
David Roper, 36, shop assistant
Religion: Protestant
Married: 17 years
Children: Janice 13, Edward 8

Angela Stone, 42, NHS VDU operator (1)
Richard Stone, 43, shift supervisor for British Coal
Religion: Protestant
Married: 17 years
Children: Paul 14, Rhona 8

Jane White, 39, home help (part-time) (4)
John White, 41, plumber
Religion: Protestant
Married: 17 years
Children: Jim 14, Philip 12, Carol 7

June Wilkins, 38, school cleaner (part-time) (1)
Bill Wilkins, 41, baker
Religion: mother – Catholic; father – Protestant
Married: 14 years (husband's second marriage)
Children: Robert 14, Gavin 7

★ denotes which school their children went to according to how the schools are numbered on the lists of schools and teachers in Appendix 1.
★★ denotes pilot sample

The mean age of mothers and fathers was 41.6 and 44.1 years respectively. The modal age of mothers and fathers was 41 and 44 years respectively. The mean and modal lengths of marriages were 18.2 years and 17 years respectively.

Social class was used as a means of dividing up the sample and was drawn from the Registrar General's classification. There were twelve (55 per cent) middle-class couples and ten (45 per cent) working-class couples. The social class of the couple was derived from the occupational title of the spouse with the highest classification. In most cases the occupational titles of the sample fitted neatly into the middle-class or working-class categories. There were three anomalous cases: two clerks and one full-time nurse (the latter also happened to be the only case where the wife had a higher classification than the husband). On balance, I decided to place them in the working-class category on the grounds that they lived in council housing. Fathers were in full-time employment with the exception of Bill Mckay who had just been laid off due to ill-health. Five (23 per cent) mothers were in full-time employment; ten (45 per cent) were in part-time employment and seven (32 per cent) were housewives.

Initially, I wanted a reasonable mix of parents of boys and girls within the 14 to 15 age range. As I have already stated, the target age was chosen more as a means of generating discussion on issues of which parents would have had some knowledge – secondary schools, sex education and curricula choice. At this stage there was a sex imbalance with fourteen couples with boys (64 per cent) and only seven with girls (32 per cent) within the target age range. But as the analysis proceeded the concept of adolescence became important. Not only had I interviewed parents of 14- and 15-year-old children, I had interviewed parents of adolescent children. If we broadened the age band to include parents with adolescent children between the ages of 13 and 18, the sex ratio of boys to girls moves from 14:7 to 14:12. Five parents with boys between the ages of 14 and 15 had girls within the broader adolescent age band.

Bibliography

ADAM SMITH INSTITUTE (1985) *The Omega File: Education Policy*, London, ASI.

ALEXANDER, R., ROSE, J. and WOODHEAD, C. (1992) *Curriculum Organisation and Classroom Practice in Primary Schools*, London, Department of Education and Science.

ALLAN, G. (1979) *A Sociology of Friendship and Kinship*, London, George Allen and Unwin.

ALLAN, G. (1980) 'A note on interviewing spouses together', *Journal of Marriage and the Family*, 42, pp. 205–10.

ALLAN, G. (1985) *Family Life*, Oxford, Blackwell.

ALLAN, G. (1989) 'Insiders and outsiders: Boundaries around the home', in ALLAN, G. and CROW, G. (eds) *Home and Family: Creating the Domestic Sphere*, Basingstoke, Macmillan.

ALLATT, P. and YEANDLE, S. (1992) *Youth Unemployment and the Family*, London, Routledge.

ALLEN, I. (1987) *Education in Sex and Personal Relationships*, London, Policy Studies Institute.

ANDERSON, D. (ed.) (1988) *Full Circle: Bringing up Children in the Post-Permissive Society*, London, Social Affairs Unit.

ARIÉS, P. (1960) *Centuries of Childhood*, Harmondsworth, Penguin.

AVIRAM, A. (1992) 'Non-lococentric education', *Educational Review*, 44, 1, pp. 3–17.

BACKETT, K. (1982) *Mothers and Fathers: A Study of the Development and Negotiation of Parental Behaviour*, London, Macmillan.

BADINTER, E. (1980) *The Myth of Motherhood*, London, Souvenir Press.

BALL, S., BOWE, R. and GEWITZ, S. (1995) 'Circuits of schooling: A sociological exploration of parental choice of school in social class contexts', *Sociological Review*, 43, 1, pp. 52–78.

BARKER, D. (1972) 'Young people and their homes: Spoiling and "keeping close" in a South Wales town', *Sociological Review*, new series, 20.

BARRETT, M. and McINTOSH, M. (1982) *The Anti-Social Family*, London, Verso.

BECHER, T., *et al.* (1981) *Policies for Educational Accountability*, London, Heinmann.

BECK, U. (1992) *Risk Society: Towards a New Modernity*, London, Sage.

BERGER, P. and BERGER, B. (1983) *The War Over the Family: Capturing the Middle Ground*, Harmondsworth, Penguin.

BERGER, P. and LUCKMAN, T. (1968) *The Social Construction of Reality*, New York, Anchor Books.

BERNARDES, J. (1985) 'Do we really know what "the family" is', in CLOSE, P. and COLLINS, R. (eds) *Family and Economy in Modern Society*, Basingstoke, Macmillan.

BERNSTEIN, B. (1975) *Class, Codes and Control Vol. 1: Theoretical Studies towards a Sociology of Language*, London, Routledge and Kegan Paul.

BEST, R. and DECKER, P. (1985) 'Pastoral care and welfare', in RIBBENS, P. (ed.) *Schooling and Welfare*, London, Falmer Press.

BOTT, E. (1964) *Family and Social Network* (second edn) London, Tavistock.

BOYSON, R. (1973) 'Order and purpose', in TURNER, B. (ed.) *Discipline in Schools*, London, War Lock Educational.

BOYSON, R. (1976) *The Crisis in Education*, London, Woburn Press.

BREHONEY, K. (1990) 'Neither rhyme nor reason: Primary schooling and the national curriculum', in FLUDE, M. and HAMMER, M. (eds) *The Education Reform Act 1988: its Origins and Implications*, London, Falmer Press.

BROADFOOT, P. (ed.) (1986) *Profiles and Records of Achievement*, London, Holt, Riehart and Winston.

BRONFENBRENNER, U. (1970) *Two Worlds of Childhood*, New York, Touchstone.

BROWN, P. (1990) 'The "third wave": Education and the ideology of parentocracy', *British Journal of the Sociology of Education*, 11, 1, pp. 65–85.

BÜCHNER, P. (1990) 'Growing up in the eighties: changes in the social biography of childhood in FRG', in CHISHOLM, L. *et al.* (eds) *Childhood, Youth and Social Change*, London, Falmer Press.

BURGESS, E. (1926) 'The family as a unity of interacting personalities', *The Family*, 7, pp. 3–9.

BURY, J. (1984) *Teenage Pregnancy in Britain*, London, Birth Control Trust.

CARLEN, P., GLEESON, D. and WARDHAUGH, J. (1992) *Truancy: The Politics of Compulsory Schooling*, Milton Keynes, Open University Press.

CENTRE FOR CONTEMPORARY CULTURAL STUDIES (1981) *Unpopular Education: Schooling and Social Democracy in England Since 1944*, London, Hutchinson.

CHEAL, D. (1991) *Family and the State of Theory*, Hemel Hempstead, Harvester Wheatsheaf.

CHITTY, C. (1989) *Towards a New Education System: The Victory of the New Right?*, London, Falmer Press.

CLARKE, M. (1986) 'Education and welfare: Issues in co-ordination and co-operation', *Pastoral Care in Education*, 4, 1, pp. 51–59.

COLEMAN, J. (1961) *The Adolescent Society*, New York, Free Press.

COLLIER, J., ROSALDO, M. and YANAGISAKO, S. (1982) 'Is there a family? new anthropological views', in B. THORNE and M. YALOM (eds) *Rethinking the Family: Some Feminist Questions*, New York, Longman.

CONNELL, R.W., ASHENDEN, D.J., KESSLER, S. and DOWSETT, G.W. (1982) *Making the Difference: Schools, Families and Social Division*, London, George Allen and Unwin.

COX, C.B. and DYSON, A.E. (eds) (1971) *The Black Papers on Education* (revised edn), London, Davis-Poynter.

CUMMINGS, C.E., *et al.* (1981) *Making the Difference: A Study of the Process of the Abolition of Corporal Punishment*, Edinburgh, SCRE.

DALEY, J. (1991) 'Stop pretending we are naturally good', *The Times*, 6th September.

DAVID, M. (1980) *The State, the Family and Education*, London, Routledge and Kegan Paul.

DAVID, M. (1993) *Parents, Gender and Education Reform*, Cambridge, Polity Press.

DAVID, M., et al. (1993) *Mothers and Education: Inside Out?*, Basingstoke, Macmillan.

DAVIS, K. (1962) 'The sociology of parent/youth conflict', in WINCH, R., MACGINNIS, R. and BARRINGER, H. (eds) *Selected Studies in Marriage and the Family*, New York, Holt, Rinehart and Winston.

DEAN, C. (1992) 'Partners or purchasers?' *Times Education Supplement*, 7th February, p. 9.

DEAN, M. (1993) 'No case for hiding in the bunker', *The Guardian*, 27th February.

DEEM, R. (1990) 'The reform of school-governing bodies: The power of the consumer over the producer?', in FLUDE, M. and HAMMER, M. (eds) *The Education Reform Act: Its Origins and Implications*, London, Falmer Press.

DENNIS, N. and ERDOS, G. (1993) *Families Without Fatherhood*, London, IEA.

DENSCOMBE, M. (1984) 'Control, controversy and the comprehensive school', in BALL, S. (ed.) *Comprehensive Schooling: A Reader*, London, Falmer Press.

DENSCOMBE, M. (1985) *Classroom Control*, London, Allen and Unwin.

DENZIN, N. (1978) *The Research Act: A Theoretical Introduction to Sociological Methods*, New York, McGraw-Hill.

DES (1989) *Discipline*, London, HMSO.

DINGWALL, R., EEKELAAR, J. and MURRAY, T. (1983) *The Protection of Children: State Intervention and Family Life*, Oxford, Blackwell.

DOCKING, J.W. (1980) *Control and Discipline in Schools: Perspectives and Approaches*, London, Harper and Row.

DONZELOT, J. (1979) *The Policing of Families*, London, Hutchinson.

DREIKURS, R., et al. (1982) *Maintaining Sanity in the Classroom* (second edn), New York, Harper and Row.

DURKHEIM, E. (1961) *Moral Education*, Glencoe, Free Press.

EATON, M. (1983) 'Mitigating circumstances: Family rhetoric', *Journal of Sociology of Law*, 11, pp. 385–400.

EMERSON, R. (1969) *Judging Delinquents*, Chicago, Chicago University.

EYSENCK, H. and NIAS, D. (1978) *Sex, Violence and the Media*, London, Maurice Temple Smith.

FARRELL, C. (1978) *My Mother Said . . . The Way Young People Learn about Sex and Birth Control*, London, Routledge and Kegan Paul.

FINCH, J. (1986) 'Pastoral care, juvenile justice and the welfare network', *Journal of Education Policy*, 1, 2, pp. 133–47.

FINKELHOR, D. (1984) *Child Sex Abuse: New Theory and Research*, New York, Free Press.

FITZ, J. (1981) 'Welfare, the family and the child', Open University Course E353, *Education, Welfare and Social Order*, Milton Keynes, Open University Press.

FLETCHER, R. (1966) *The Family and Marriage in Britain*, Harmondsworth, Penguin.

FLUDE, M. and HAMMER, M. (1990) *The Education Reform Act 1988: Its Origins and Implications*, London, Falmer Press.

FOUCAULT, M. (1976) *The History of Sexuality*, Harmondsworth, Penguin.

FOUCAULT, M. (1977) *Discipline and Punish*, Harmondsworth, Penguin.

FRIEDMAN, M. (1962) *Free to Choose*, Harmondsworth, Penguin.

GAGNON, J. and SIMON, W. (1973) *Sexual Conduct*, Chicago, Aldine Publishing Company.

GERTH, H. and MILLS, C.W. (1948) *From Max Weber*, London, Routledge and Kegan Paul.

GIDDENS, A. (1976) *New Rules of Sociological Method*, London, Hutchinson.

GIDDENS, A. (1984) *The Constitution of Society*, Cambridge, Polity Press.

GIDDENS, A. (1991) *Modernity and Self Identity*, Cambridge, Policy Press.

GIL, D. (1971) 'Violence against children', *Journal of Marriage and the Family*, 33.

GITTINS, D. (1985) *The Family in Question*, Basingstoke, Macmillan.

GOFFMAN, E. (1969) *The Presentation of Self in Everyday Life*, London, Allen Lane.

GOFFMAN, E. (1972) *Encounters: Two Studies in the Sociology of Interaction*, Harmondsworth, Penguin.

GOLDMAN, R. and GOLDMAN, J. (1982) *Children's Sexual Thinking*, London, Routledge.

GOLDTHORPE, J.E. (1987) *Family Life in Western Societies*, Cambridge, Cambridge University Press.

GOODE, W. (1971) 'Force in the family', *Journal of Marriage and the Family*, 33.

GREENFIELD, P. (1984) *Mind and Media: The Effects of TV, Video Games and Computers*, London, Fontana.

GUBRIUM, J. and HOLSTEIN, J. (1990) *What is Family?*, Mayfield, California.

HALL, S. (1983) 'The great moving right show', in HALL, S. and JACQUES, M. (eds) *The Politics of Thatcherism*, London, Lawrence Wishart.

HAMMERSLEY, M. (1990) *Classroom Ethnography*, Milton Keynes, Open University Press.

HARDY, J. and VIELER-PORTER, C. (1990) 'Race, schooling and the 1988 Education Reform Act', in FLUDE, M. and HAMMER, M. (eds) *The Education Reform Act 1988: Its Origins and Implications*, London, Falmer Press.

HARGREAVES, A. (1979) 'Strategies, decisions and control: Interaction in a middle school classroom', in EGGLESTON, J. (ed.) *Teacher Decision-Making in the Classroom*, London, Routledge.

HARGREAVES, A. (1984) 'The significance of classroom strategies', in HARGREAVES, A. and WOODS, P. (eds) *Classrooms and Staffrooms*, Milton Keynes, Open University Press.

HARGREAVES, A. (1986) 'Record breakers?', in BROADFOOT, P. (ed.) *Profiles and Records of Achievement*, London, Holt, Reinhart and Winston.

HARGREAVES, A. and REYNOLDS, D. (1990) 'Decomprehensivisation', in HARGREAVES, A. and REYNOLDS, D. (eds) *Educational Policies: Controversies and Critiques*, London, Falmer Press.

HARGREAVES, A. (1994) *Changing Teachers, Changing Times*, London, Cassell.

HARGREAVES, D. (1994) 'The new professionalism: the synthesis of professional and institutional development', *Teaching and Teacher Education*, 10, 4, pp. 423–38.

HARRIS, C.C. (1969) *The Family*, London, George Allen and Unwin.

HARRIS, C.C. (1980) 'The changing relation between family and societal form in western society', in ANDERSON, M. (ed.) *Sociology of the Family* (second edn), Harmondsworth, Penguin.

HARRIS, C.C. (1983) *The Family and Industrial Society*, London, George Allen and Unwin.

HARRIS, R. and WEBB, D. (1987) *Welfare, Power and Juvenile Justice*, London, Tavistock.

HOLMAN, R. (1988) *Putting Families First: Prevention and Child Care*, Basingstoke, Macmillan.

HOME OFFICE (1992) *Crime, Justice and Protecting the Public*, HMSO.

HOOD-WILLIAMS, J. (1990) 'Patriarchy for children: on the stability of power relations in children's lives', in CHISHOLM, L. *et al.* (eds) *Childhood, Youth and Social Change*, London, Falmer Press.

JAMIESON, L. (1987) 'Theories of family development and the experience of being brought up', *Sociology*, 21, 4.

JAMIESON, L. and CORR, H. (1990) *'Earning Your Keep': Self Reliance and Family Obligation*, ESRC 16–19 Initiative Occasional Paper, 30.

JOHNSON, D. (1983) *Family and School*, London, Croom Helm.

JOHNSON, D., *et al.* (1980) *Secondary Schools and the Welfare Network*, London, George Allen and Unwin.

JOHNSON, M. (1987) *Discipline in School: A Review of 'Causes' and 'Cures'*, Edinburgh, SCRE.

LA FONTAINE, J. (1990) *Child Sex Abuse*, Oxford, Polity Press.

LAING, R.D. and ESTERSON, A. (1970) *Sanity, Madness and the Family*, second edition, London, Pelican.

LANG, P. and MARLAND, M. (eds) (1985) *New Directions in Pastoral Care*, Oxford, Blackwell.

LAREAU, A. (1989) *Home Advantage: Social Class and Parental Intervention*, London, Falmer Press.

LASCH, C. (1977) *Haven in a Heartless World: The Family Besieged*, New York, Basic Books.

LASCH, C. (1979) *The Culture of Narcissism*, London, Abacus.

LEE, C. (1983) *The Ostrich Position: Sex, Schooling and Mystification*, London, Writers and Readers Cooperative Society.

LEES, S. (1993) *Sugar and Spice*, Harmondsworth, Penguin.

LEONARD, D. (1980) *Sex and Generation*, London, Tavistock.

LEVITAS, R. (ed.) (1986) *The Ideology of the New Right*, Oxford, Polity Press.

LEWIS, C. and O'BRIEN, M. (eds) (1987) *Reassessing Fatherhood*, London, Sage.

LONGFORD COMMITTEE (1972) *Pornography: The Longford Report*, London, Coronet.

MACBETH, A. (1984) *The Child Between: A Report on School–Family Relations in the Countries of the European Community*, Brussels, EEC.

MACBETH, A. (1989) *Involving Parents: Effective Parent–Teacher Relations*, Oxford, Heinemann.

McPHERSON, A. (1983) 'An angle on the giest: Persistence and change in the Scottish educational tradition', in HUMES, W. and PATERSON, H. (eds) *Scottish Culture and Scottish Education 1800–1900*, Edinburgh, John Donald.

MCPHERSON, A. and RAAB, C. (1988) *Governing Education: A Sociology of Policy Since 1945*, Edinburgh, Edinburgh University Press.

MAHER, P. (ed.) (1987) *Child Abuse: the Educational Perspective*, Oxford, Blackwell.

MEASOR, L. (1989) 'Are you coming to see some dirty films today? sex education and adolescent sexuality', in HOLLY, L. (ed.) *Girls and Sexuality*, Milton Keynes, Open University.

MEIGHAN, R. (1989a) 'Preface', *Educational Review*, 41, 2.

MEIGHAN, R. (1989b) 'The parents and the schools', *Educational Review*, 14, 2, pp. 105–112.

MEIKLE, R. (1980) 'A need to certify the foundation child', in *Times Education Supplement, Scotland*, 24th October, pp. 12–13.

MEYER, P. (1977) *The Child and the State: The Intervention of the State in Family Life*, Cambridge, Cambridge University Press.

MILLER, L. (1990) 'Violent families and the rhetoric of harmony', *British Journal of Sociology*, 41, 2, 263–88.

MISHRA, R. (1984) *The Welfare State in Crisis*, Brighton, Wheatsheaf.

MORGAN, D.H.J. (1985) *The Family, Politics and Social Theory*, London, Routledge and Kegan Paul.

MOUNT, F. (1982) *The Subversive Family*, London, Allen and Unwin.

NEILL, A. (1962) *Summerhill*, Harmondsworth, Penguin.

NEWSON, J. and NEWSON, E. (1963) *Patterns of Infant Care*, London, Allen and Unwin.

NEWSON, J. and NEWSON, E. (1968) *Four Years Old in an Urban Community*, London, Allen and Unwin.

NEWSON, J. and NEWSON, E. (1976) *Seven Years Old in the Home Environment*, London, Allen and Unwin.

OAKELY, A. (1974) *Housewife*, Harmondsworth, Penguin.

PARSONS, T. (1949) *Essays in Sociological Theory*, Glencoe, Free Press.

PARSONS, T. (1965) *Social Structure and Personality*, London, Free Press.

PARSONS, T. and BALES, R.F. (1956) *Family, Socialisation and Interaction Process*, London, Routledge and Kegan Paul.

PARTON, N. (1985) *The Politics of Child Abuse*, Basingstoke, Macmillan.

PATERSON, F. (1989) *Out of Place: Public Policy and the Emergence of Truancy*, London, Falmer Press.

POLLARD, A. (1982) 'A model of classroom coping strategies', *British Journal of the Sociology of Education*, 6, 1.

POPAY, J., *et al.* (1983) *One Parent Families*, Occasional Paper no. 12, London, Study Commission on Families.

POPENOE, D. (1988) *Disturbing the Nest*, New York, Aldine de Gruyter.

POWER, S. (1991) 'Pastoral care as curriculum discourse: a study in the reformation of "academic" schooling', *International Journal of Sociology of Education*, 1, pp. 193–208.

PRENDERGAST, S. and PROUT, A. (1987) *Knowing and Learning about Parenthood*, Cambridge, Health Education Authority.

PRESTON, B. (1994) 'Patten spells out code to tighten school discipline', *The Times*, January 5th, p. 1.

PROUT, A. (1988) ' "Off Sick": Mothers' accounts of school sickness absence', *Sociological Review*, 36, 4, pp, 765–89.

PYKE, N. (1992) 'Into the exclusion zone', *Times Education Supplement*, 26th June, p. 14.

RAPOPORT, R. and RAPOPORT, R. (1976) *Dual-Career Families Re-examined*, London, Martin Robertson.

RAPOPORT, R., RAPOPORT, R. and STRELITZ, Z. (1977) *Fathers, Mothers and Others*, London, Routledge and Kegan Paul.

REYNOLDS, D. and SULLIVAN, M. (1979) 'Bringing the school back in', in BARTON, L. and MEIGHAN, R. (eds) *Schools, Pupils and Deviance*, Nafferton, Driffield.

RIBBINS, P. (ed.) (1985) *Schooling and Welfare*, London, Falmer Press.

RIBBENS, J. (1993) 'Standing by the school gate – the boundaries of maternal authority?', in DAVID, M. *et al.* (eds) *Mothers and Education: Inside Out?*, Basingstoke Macmillan.

RIESMAN, D. (1950) *The Lonely Crowd*, New Haven, Yale University Press.

RIESS, M. (1993) 'What are the aims of sex education?', *Cambridge Journal of Education*, 23, 2, pp. 125–36.

SCHOFIELD, M. (1965) *The Sexual Behaviour of Young People*, London, Longman.

SCRUTON, R. (1980) *The Meaning of Conservatism*, Harmondsworth, Penguin.

SEABROOK, J. (1982) *Working Class Childhood*, London, Golancz.

SEX EDUCATION FORUM (1988) *Statement on Teaching about Homosexuality*, London, National Children's Bureau.

SHARPE, S. (1976) *Just Like a Girl: How Girls Learn to be a Women*, Harmondsworth, Penguin.

SHARP, R. and GREEN, A. (1975) *Education and Social Control*, London, Routledge, and Kegan Paul.

SHAW, J. (1981) 'In loco parentis: a relationship between parent, state and child', in DALE, R. *et al.* (eds) *Politics, Patriarchy and Practice*, London, Falmer Press.

SPENCER, C. (1990) 'Childhood and public life: reaffirming biographical divisions', *Social Problems*, 37, 3, pp. 390–402.

STANWORTH, M. (1981) *Gender and Schooling*, London, Hutchinson.

STEARS, D. and CLIFT, S. (1991) 'AIDS education in secondary schools', *Education and Health*, 9, 2, pp. 23–6.

STRAUSS, M., GELLES, R. and STEINMETZ, S. (1980) *Behind Closed Doors: Violence in the American Family*, Newbury Park, Sage.

SZASZ, T. (1980) *Sex: Facts, Frauds and Follies*, Oxford, Blackwell.

TOOMEY, D. (1989) 'Linking class and gender inequality: The family and schooling', *British Journal of Sociology of Education*, 10, 4.

TRIBE, K. (1978) *Land, Labour and Economic Discourse*, London, Routledge and Kegan Paul.

UTTING, D. (1993) 'How families can prevent delinquency', *The Independent on Sunday*, 28th February.

VÁSQUEZ, A. and MARTÍNEZ, I. (1992) 'Paris–Barcelona: invisible interactions in the classroom', *Anthropology & Education Quarterly*, 23, pp. 291–312.

WALKERDINE, V. (1990) *Schoolgirl Fictions*, London, Verso.

WALLACE, W. (1993) 'And baby makes two', *Times Education Supplement*, October 1st, pp. 1–2.

WARD, D. (1994) ' "Basic" Patten list baffles head whose tough rules already work', *The Guardian*, January 5th, p. 2.

WEBER, M. (1968) *Economy and Society*, vol. 1, New York, Bedminster Press.

WEEKS, J. (1981) *Sex, Politics and Society: The Regulation of Sexuality Since 1800*, London, Longman.

WEST, A. and VARLAAM, A. (1991) 'Choosing a secondary school: Parents of junior school children', *Educational Research*, 33, 1, pp. 22–30.

WEXLER, J., *et al.* (1992) *Becoming Somebody: Toward a Social Psychology of School*, London, Falmer Press.

WILLIS, P. (1977) *Learning to Labour*, Aldershot, Saxon House.

WILSON, B.R. (1962) 'The teacher's role – a sociological analysis', *British Journal of Sociology*, 13, pp. 15–32.

WILSON, H. and HERBERT, G. (1978) *Parents and Children in the Inner City*, London, Routledge.

WOLFE, R. (1962) 'Power and authority in the family', in WINCH, R., MACGINNIS, R. and BARRINGER, H. (eds) *Selected Studies in Marriage and the Family*, New York, Holt, Rinehart and Winston.

WOLPE, A. (1988) *Within School Walls: The Role of Discipline, Sexuality and the Curriculum*, London, Routledge.

WOODS, P. (ed.) (1980) *Teacher Strategies*, London, Croom Helm.

WOODS, P. (1988) 'A strategic view of parental participation', *Journal of Educational Policy*, 3, 4, pp. 323–34.

WYNESS, M. (1990) 'Review of Anderson', in DIGBY. (ed.) *Full Circle: Bringing up Children in the Post-Permissive Society*, in *The Sociological Review*, 38, 1, pp. 189–192.

WYNESS, M. (1992) 'Schooling and the normalisation of sex talk within the home', *British Journal of the Sociology of Education*, 13, 1, pp. 89–104.

WYNESS, M. (1994) 'Keeping tabs on an uncivil society: positive parental control', *Sociology*, 28, 1, pp. 193–209.

WYNESS, M. (1995, forthcoming) 'Schooling, welfare and the policing of parents', *British Journal of Sociology of Education*, 16, 3, pp. 373–87.

WYNESS, M. (1996) 'Les possibilistés de l'ethnographie et la probléme de la vie privée: les rapports des parents et des enseignants sur les "parents responsables" ', in VÁSQUEZ, A. and MARTÍNEZ, I. (eds) *Perspectives ethnographieques dans l'analyse de l'éducation des années 90: La socialisation à l'Ecole et l'Intégration des Minorités*, Madrid, Infancìa y Aprendizaje, forthcoming.

ZARETSKY, E. (1982) 'The place of the family in the origins of the welfare state', in THORNE, B. and YALOM, M. (eds) *Rethinking the Family: Some Feminist Questions*, New York, Longman.

Index